Off the Grid Homes

Off the Grid Homes

Case Studies for Sustainable Living

Lori Ryker with photographs by Audrey Hall

Gibbs Smith, Publisher
TO ENRICH AND INSPIRE HUMANKIND

Salt Lake City | Charleston | Santa Fe | Santa Barbara

First Edition
11 10 09 08 07   5 4 3 2 1

Text © 2007 Lori Ryker
Photographs © 2007 Audrey Hall, except as noted on page 123
Drawings © 2007 Tripp Lewton, pages 40-41, 52-56, 70-71, 86-87, 102–3

Published by
Gibbs Smith, Publisher
PO Box 667
Layton, Utah 84041

Orders: 1.800.835.4993
www.gibbs-smith.com

Designed by Debra McQuiston
Printed and bound in Hong Kong

Library of Congress Cataloging-in-Publication Data

Ryker, Lori, 1963-
  Off the grid homes : case studies for sustainable living / Lori Ryker ; photographs by Audrey Hall. — 1st ed.
    p. cm.
  Includes index.
  ISBN-13: 978-1-58685-689-2
  ISBN-10: 1-58685-689-8
  1. Architecture, Domestic—Environmental aspects. 2. Architecture and energy conservation. I. Title.

NA7117.3.R95 2007
720'.47—dc22

2006029423

To Brett Nave for his support, encouragement, and clear thinking, which have helped me to accomplish this work.

Thanks to everyone in my office for assisting during the research, development, and writing of the book. Thanks to Tripp Lewton for going on the journey with me to simplify and graphically translate the energy systems for the readers. Thanks to the architects who gave more than they are used to in order to fulfill the technical aspects of the project descriptions, to Professor Tom Wood who worked through the diagrams with me, and to Mike Ketchum who took the time to explain the technical side of geothermal systems.

contents

preface

In *Off the Grid: Modern Homes + Alternative Energy*, I introduced the basic systems of alternative energy as well as the general conditions that are required to incorporate such technologies into a well-designed home. With this book, I delve more deeply into alternative systems and technologies in order for the reader to understand the diversity of their applications and how to determine the appropriate use for a given location and goal. Perhaps some day when this book is gathering dust on a shelf we will no longer be referring to these ideas and strategies as "alternative" but simply know them as mainstream, conventional ways of living on the Earth. That will be a great day.

Introduction:

Coming to terms with off the grid

ENERGY CONSERVATION AND A HEALTHIER PLANET

In the 1970s, there was a period, inspired by the oil shortage in the United States, in which there was an initial push to bring alternative energies into the mainstream. While the impetus for the push was brought on by a concern for the ability of modern civilization to continue to develop and expand at the rate it had and concern about excessive rates of energy consumption, there was also naive optimism among alternative-energy supporters that the time had come for clean energy and a cleaner planet. Within a few years, the political global dynamic that drove the oil shortage created new oil resources, resulting in the public and private sectors' temporary disinterest in alternative-energy sources. Twenty-five years have passed since the oil crisis of the '70s, and we are again witnessing a potential global energy crisis. This time it is not only political differences that are responsible for the crisis, but a population explosion and the greater energy demands of industrialized countries. Perhaps this time the supporters of alternative clean energy will see their vision secure a foothold in the mainstream of Western society. Maybe this time there will not only be strategies of conservation employed but clean technologies, recently called off-the-grid technologies, that will be incorporated for a healthier planet.

The term *off the grid* became popular in the early 1990s to describe homes and other buildings that employ alternative-energy-source solutions rather than main line, municipal-tied energy sources to provide power. Early in the development

This residence, located in Ukiah, California, is 100 percent off the grid. The home's design engages its owners with the cycles of the Earth through passive heating and cooling.

of alternative living lifestyles, such solutions were believed to be only applicable for those people living in remote locations and/or cooperative communities. As the term *off the grid* gained popularity with a new generation of energy consumers, it grew into a catch phrase that conveyed living environments that are completely disconnected and without reliance on a public infrastructure. Without a clearly articulated definition, *off the grid* by default came to mean no reliance on publicly supplied energy, sewer, or water. In the past few years, the term *off the grid* or *off-grid* has found great support on Web sites. Even the popular Wikipedia site has a listing for *off the grid:* "a method of construction that relies on renewable energy sources rather than traditional public utility sources provided by the utility "grid.""*

As I began researching homes that fit the off-the-grid qualification, it became clear to me that there are many aspects of energy and resource independence that are applicable to this term. For instance, rainwater collection, used to reduce a homeowner's reliance on municipal water, provides a component of off-the-grid living, yet the house may not be 100 percent off the grid. In the same way, someone may elect to integrate a photovoltaic (PV) system that is large enough to support all of their electrical-energy needs but live within the city limits, which requires them to remain tied to the municipal infrastructure. They may not be living 100 percent off the grid, but they have found a way to produce their own energy while continuing to live within the density of the city. As a happy consequence, their intertie to the power grid may allow them to share their "extra" clean energy created by their PV system with their neighbors through a buy-back program. In the spirit of conservation, some off-the-grid homes gain independence due to a homeowner's commitment to low technology systems in a remote location, such as a cabin that has no running water or power. Long-term planning may even allow focused homeowners to phase out their reliance upon the municipal system to fit their available funding. One may start with water collection, later add a solar hot-water heater, and eventually add a PV system and a gray-water system—with the final goal of rendering their home life fully independent from the grid.

Off the grid no longer means a system that is 100 percent independent from municipal ties, but it instead defines the use of sources and strategies that integrate one or more systems that are not reliant upon the municipal infrastructure. While we may dream of a day when we are no longer reliant upon nonrenewable energy systems or systems of disposal that are polluting, toxic, and degrading to our environment, our ability to participate in the preservation of the environment by incorporating and integrating off-the-grid practices is possible today. The choice to integrate off-the-grid systems into our lives not only provides a cleaner lifestyle, but such choices also act as dynamic political statements that can spur the development of cleaner municipal infrastructures from which we can all benefit.

As the advanced world is faced with declining oil reserves and a growing population that recognizes the consequences of our actions upon the Earth, not only individuals but entire communities and even large energy cooperatives are developing cleaner energy practices. From individual

homeowners who have their own PV arrays that work together as a small, clean energy plant when joined in a grid-intertie system, to a statewide energy cooperative that commits to the development of large-scale wind turbines for energy production, cleaner energy and a healthier Earth are within our reach as long as we remain attentive and committed to a vision of a world in which our own perceived needs are not always placed first.

THE FORMAT OF THIS BOOK
The next section of this book, "Setting the Stage: Creating Visions for a Sustainable World," presents three landmark case studies supported by grants and public funding that are rich and thoughtful in their designs and incorporations of off-the-grid technologies and systems. This section is followed by six in-depth case studies of homes that present what is possible today in the private sector.

Opposite: Rainwater collected off a roof into an above-ground cistern provides a visual reference to measure seasonal rainfall.

Right: This rooftop PV array not only provides power to the home, but also acts as a sculptural complement to the rooftop.

Each case study presents a home that is designed to require less of the Earth's nonrenewable resources, consume cleaner energy, and output fewer pollutants. The goal of the case study format is to communicate how the particular home is designed as an integrated whole with these goals in mind. Rather than present the technologies and strategies in an itemized format, these projects demonstrate a range of integrated possibilities located in different environments. While you may not find a home that exactly represents your environment or lifestyle, you may recognize similarities that can help you begin to craft your own vision of cleaner living. In addition, by considering the relationship between the size of the home and the size and types of systems presented through each case study, you should be able to gain a basic alternative-energy vocabulary and a general understanding of what you can expect from an integrated home and alternative-energy system.

Within the case study section you will find diagrams and explanations of the variations of the system employed, which will help you gain a better understanding of the system's potential applications and performance in different conditions. There are also general diagrams that explain how a system works. By no means do the projects represented within this book present an exhaustive study of off-the-grid systems. Rather, they should provide you with an understanding of the value of developing a long-term vision of energy use through an integrated design, which employs alternative technologies and requires a redefinition of lifestyle.

*See http://en.wikipedia.org/wiki/Off_the_grid.

Setting the stage: Creating visions for a sustainable world

Homes are expressions of collected day-to-day experiences. They provide a place of refuge and memory making. From within our dwellings, our lives unfold and are invented, while personal beliefs are explored and expressed. Rituals are created and reenacted daily, weekly, or monthly, responding to our interpretations of how to live in the world. Holidays are given their context from within our homes, entwining our sense of an event within a particular place. Homes have the ability to express and embody an understanding of ourselves and our relationship to the world around us. They express who we are, who we want to be, and how we will be remembered.

Throughout the world, we find vastly different sensibilities toward living expressed in homes. From simple to complex, the evolution of our homes is not only a response to our interest in our well-being but is also a response to our ability to put into action our beliefs. From simple dwellings that first served to separate us from the harshness of the outside world, we have evolved our homes to respond to our sense of reality through developing cultural visions supported by materials, construction techniques, and evolving technologies. Whether rented or owned, freestanding or multiunit, rural or urban, homes provide an opening to express a vision of the world as we understand it.

The opportunity for a home to provide more than shelter, to provide a personal expression of the self, is gained when a culture prospers, which means the culture has free time, extra money, or both. The modern world prospered through the past few hundred years, providing more and more people with the opportunity to express themselves through their homes.[1]

One of the greatest periods of transformations in the expression of homes in the Western world came after World War II. After the depression of the 1930s and rationing during the war, the United States and Europe, in particular, were ready to move beyond the years of conservation and concern, both in cultural expression and personal consumption.

During the war, a change in lifestyle began that set in motion a social evolution that transformed modern culture. For instance, with the primary wage earner gone, families could not retain their domestic help. The middle class, in particular, which had employed cooks and maidservants before the war, was faced with performing all of the domestic work in their homes themselves. Women grew accustom to taking on responsibilities that would have typically been left to their husbands. In addition, most women who were not directly involved in the war had grown accustom to a multitasking lifestyle in which they were engaged in raising their families, working out of the home for the first time, and making decisions on their own. The formality of the pre-World War II conventions of culture found in the United States and elsewhere gave way to blurring roles between men and women, crossovers in responsibilities, and a more relaxed style of living supported by the ideals of independence, freedom, and equality that were rapidly spreading across the Western world.[2]

The modern world, led by the United States, had a desire to leave behind the challenging decades of the 1930s and '40s and cast itself as a society of prosperity, leisure, and independence. Such intent had great effects on the evolution of the home. Homes provided the perfect context from which to materialize these developing ideals and evolving sense of reality, as well as to create opportunities for them to be experienced. The conventions for home life were evolving. Formalities and strong divisions between public and private qualities of life were blurring, conventional roles and preferences of men and women were being challenged, and social and cultural boundaries were breaking down. As new ways to express potential freedoms were explored, new materials, tools, and technologies also became key considerations for remaking cultural expression. For these reasons and more, how homes were built, finished, furnished, and powered became a necessary and powerful expression in people's lives. Yet since aspects of architecture evolve over time, responding to cultural developments and technological advancements, learning of their availability can be challenging.

Above: This remodeled rooftop in Seattle provides a challenging dialogue to its neighbors: a roof can provide more than shelter; it can also generate energy.

Right: In the spirit of the case study houses, this California house opens out onto a courtyard with exterior living spaces.

TRANSFORMING THE HOME

In the 1940s, John Entenza, who was the owner and editor of the journal *Arts and Architecture (AA)*, began the Case Study House program. According to Esther McCoy, the *AA* developed out of "a period of strong social conscience, a reflection of the idealism and Puritanism of the Depression and war years when architecture was first of all a social art."[3] The Case Study House program sprang from Entenza's belief in the necessity of demonstrating the possibilities of a new era of expression for living. He found these expressions in the provocative visions of the young architects of California. The program also provided an ideal format for the general public to explore and learn about architecture.

Entenza recognized great changes in the materials, methods of construction, and technologies available to architecture. He believed the Case Study House program would support the development of a critical body of work, relevant to the time, which would challenge the seemingly endless romanticizing of architectural styles. The house also provided a model that could be easily explored due to its scale and its adoptability by the general public. The initial concepts

Opposite: A well-developed exterior space allows people to live outside as well as inside. At the same time, large sliding doors open to virtually erase the boundary of inside from outside.

Above: The small footprint of this house allows the homeowners to live fully off the grid with a small PV array and solar hot-water heater.

of exploration for study included pragmatism, service, standardization, and modular prototypes. For the first phase of the program Entenza purchased five acres upon which to build a series of homes, and a legacy was born.

The case study houses were sited in Los Angeles, a place of progressive mentality and expression. Additionally, California's mild climate provided an ideal opportunity for an architecture that came to express the evolving cultural ideals of freedom, dissolving of formalities, and the creation of the casual lifestyle. Conventional houses defined by perimeter enclosure walls, resulting in box-like characteristics, divided by a series of rooms on the interior, gave way to interconnected horizontal and vertical planes with large openings that allowed rooms to flow together into loose and ambiguous spaces, providing opportunities for living to spread from inside to out. The houses had openness to them. Undefined interiors expressed in newly developed materials and systems of steel frames, concrete floors, plywood, and sheet cladding transformed people's assumptions and expectations of architecture. The new spatial expression, materials, methods of construction, and technologies

incorporated in them were embraced by a community that was not afraid to experiment with their evolving sense of self. Upon completion, the homes were opened for the public to visit and later sold to generate funding for the next phase of the program.

Arts and Architecture spread this new vision of living across the United States, Europe, and elsewhere through its publication of the case study houses. The program, which ran from 1945–62, was one of the most successful educational methods for transforming cultural expression in the last century. The Eames House, one of the first built during the program, remains one of the most influential pieces of architecture produced during this era. Its legacy is recognizable from California to Pennsylvania, from Australia to Finland, in homes that are open in plan, visually different from their neighbors, and that often follow the tenets of expression of California's climate: large glass walls and sliding glass doors, thin mullion profiles, low pitched roofs, and garden court spaces.

Entenza's case study homes ran parallel to the expanding and stabilizing economy of the modern world, which made the adoption of these new visions easily incorporable into suburban neighborhoods and communities across the world. A large and expanding population of the Western world was capable of redefining the vision of themselves through the qualities of leisure and prosperity, a vision that held strong through the 1970s.

TRANSFORMING THE WORLD

As the modern world gained affluency and freedom through leisure, ramifications were felt across the Earth. Affluency not only had an effect on the evolution of homes, towns, and cities, but also on what was valued, consumed, and acquired. The desire to modernize not only resulted in more progressive living environments, homes that were equipped with mechanical air-conditioning and heating, refrigerators, stoves, dishwashers, interior lighting, trash compactors, televisions, ice makers, and computers, but also an Earth that became overly taxed.

Leisure and affluency had come to mean not only the relaxed life but a life of commodified consumption. The presentation and packaging of everything from material goods to travel experiences transformed the way modern society saw themselves in the world and participated in it. The conservative life of pre–World War II was answered

by excess, overuse, and expansion that affected the Earth in terms of its resources, quality of environments, and autonomy of societies. A disparity grew between those who could afford to live a life of extreme leisure and those who could not. The disparity could be measured in the amount of energy that was used in particular parts of the world, the amount of natural resources that were dedicated to gaining energy and producing material goods, as well as the amount of land that was changed from healthy to polluted, or unoccupied to occupied.

Projecting what would occur through development, expansion and rebuilding after World War II, visionary thinker Buckminster Fuller recognized the mid-century situation and its potential devastation for Earth and humanity. By 1944, his explorations and experiments were impacting the thoughts of millions of people across the globe. A long-lasting proposition was his invention of the geodesic dome, a system of construction that relied on structural members in tension rather than compression, which was exhibited in *La Triennale di Milano* in 1954. The dome supported his mission by "doing more with less."[4] At the same time of the exhibit, Fuller was also developing a lifelong treatise he

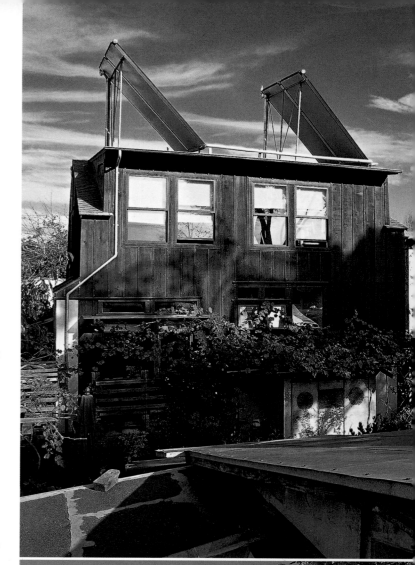

Opposite, above: A PV array can be added to an existing in-town home in a grid-intertie to reduce the home's reliance on nonrenewable resources.

Opposite, below: A rooftop greenhouse not only adds a sculptural component to a rooftop, but also provides a place to grow a garden of edible plants.

Above: Most mechanical rooms look unapproachable to a lay person. This system includes a PV inverter added to a pre-existing mechanical system. While it may appear complicated, such an addition is quite simple for most electricians.

called *Comprehensive Anticipatory Design,* which described "the effective application of the principles of science to the conscious design of our total environment in order to help make the Earth's finite resources meet the needs of humanity without disrupting the ecological processes of the planet."[5] Fuller's vision spurred a different way of looking at the world and humanity's effects upon the planet. By the 1970s, a new vision of potential was being cast as conscientious observers recognized the depletion of resources and environmental pollution as well as social inequality across the Earth. What became clear to many is that the prevalent ideological rendering of leisure comes at a price. The question that was asked was whether modern societies were willing to continue to exchange the health of the world for the qualities of leisure to which they had become accustom. What many concluded was that a little more human effort, consideration, and ingenuity could provide a more enriched life and better place to live for all.

THE NEW CASE STUDY HOUSES

Attempting to come to terms with the potential crisis that could be the future, the world's population is once again exploring who we can become and how we should live in the world. A new paradigm of living is being drawn, created, and envisioned. Holistic and interdependent concepts are challenging the twentieth-century mentality of leisure, freedom, and prosperity. Explorations, tests, and new models for living in the world are developing. As before, case studies are being employed as a way for the public to understand the potential for a new expression in living. In the realm of architecture and technology, case studies can still provide a testing ground for exploring and experiencing the possibilities. They capture the ideals of an evolving cultural vision through a tangible and testable model. They act as a looking glass to what living in the world could become.

Architectural case studies can demonstrate ways for living less resource-reliant lives and serve as the common departure point of a growing collective understanding of sustainable living. Evolving technologies, materials, and techniques that have less or minimal impact on the planet can be explored and studied in architectural designs that are specific to a particular environmental and sociocultural condition. A key advantage to these new case studies is that they can be found all over the world, serving as particular responses to particular locales. They are available for more people to experience.

While there has not been an effective private sponsor of case study houses since Entenza, other sponsors have taken on the responsibility for helping to remake the sense of ourselves in a world that is quickly faltering under our pressures of prosperity. Today, the typical case study home is sponsored by federal grants, businesses, and not-for-profit organizations. These projects are not built for a specific homeowner but respond to a generalized program most often to be experienced as an interactive exhibit. In some instances, the projects are later sold to a private party or endowed to a research program.

As we reenvision ourselves in the world and attempt to modify our consumption of the Earth, technologies and energy systems have grown into key considerations. Case studies have the opportunity to present the newest, most exciting, and engaging material and technical possibilities available in the realm of architecture, a realm that is often unobtainable in its comprehensiveness by the general public. Many of the applications demonstrated are not expensive, but they are innovative in the use of materials and techniques. The incorporation of these innovations allows us to experience and evaluate what is possible within practicable terms and what is possible and desirable within the expectations of our own lives.

Three landmark case studies completed between 1992 and 1997 serve to demonstrate the degree to which we may integrate our lives sensitively with the world. Each explores aspects of sustainable design and alternative energy specific to the place in which they are sited. Each is a locally specific demonstration of what is possible when the cultural ideals of sustainable living are made specific. These case studies present a more healthful and sustainable way to live on the Earth through responsive architecture. Without a doubt, these new case studies have directly or indirectly influenced the homes that are found in the main body of this book. They also serve as models for new homeowners across the globe that take to heart the vision of sustainable living by personally financing their alternative-energy home from

Opposite: This residence not only incorporates alternative technologies, but is also built of straw bales, an agricultural by-product.

Above: The Monier house has large operable windows and doors that allow summer breezes to flow through the home. The metal ceiling allows light to bounce back into the space.

which their local communities can learn. The technology and strategies employed in these three examples are fully integrated into the design of the homes, demonstrating the need to consider architecture as a symbiotic whole in order to fully take advantage of the possibilities and live more resource-conserving lives.

Monier House of the Future. In 1992, the award-winning design created by Kimberly Ackert and Robert Dawson-Browne, and sponsored by the Monier Corporation of Perth, Australia, was completed. The project was conceived as a case study house, which would be sold a year later to a private client. Designed to operate fully independent from the energy and municipal grids, the Monier House has a comprehensive energy strategy that incorporates active and passive environmental systems. Active systems include those that require a mechanical system supplied by generated power to operate, such as radiant heat and forced air. Passive systems are those that do not require mechanization to work but that may require human intervention, such as collecting rainwater or

using operable windows to ventilate a house. With the design intent of the Monier House focusing on active and passive system integration, a primary lesson of the home is that a comfortable living environment is achieved when the active components are working with the passive components. The active system, which includes a wind turbine, photovoltaic (PV) panels, and rainwater collection, supports the minimal energy requirements of the house. A strategy of minimal active energy works in a climate such as Perth's, which has mild to cool winters and warm to hot summers. The energy output is complemented by the passive consideration of the sun, wind, and thermal capacity of the home's construction materials. Surrounding tree cover and hills on the four-acre site serve to cool and channel the summer breezes. The result is a house that is cool in summer and warm in winter.

The home is divided into two volumes by an exterior linear court space running east to west that distinguishes public living space from private spaces and allows for passive winter solar gain and ventilation into

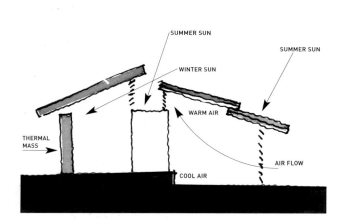

SUMMER SUN

WINTER SUN

SUMMER SUN

WARM AIR

THERMAL MASS

AIR FLOW

COOL AIR

and through both volumes. The court between the two volumes splays open to the west, orienting the circulation of the home toward a view to the city of Perth. A secondary axis through the home, running north to south, creates a circulation path between the carport and entry vestibule, drawing in a view of a seasonal pond. The open north facade allows the sun to enter in the winter, heating both volumes during the day, particularly the public volume that has an expansive, operable window wall. Louvers along the court side of the public-space volume allow for hot air to escape at the highest point of the ceiling. A long rammed earth wall runs the length of the house, protecting the private volume from winter winds. Deep roof eaves, which serve to block the summer sun from entering the interior of the house, create outdoor spaces along the north face of the home, extending the living area to outside.

The materials of the Monier House are simple and available in this region of Australia, adding to the regional specificity of the home and its sustainable qualities due to minimal transportation costs. Corrugated metal, a common material of the Australian homesteaders, encloses the soffit of the eaves and extends into the ceilings of the house, providing for the bouncing of light into the rooms. The rammed earth wall, built from the locally available iron-rich dirt, also provides a heat sink during the winter that collects solar heat for the house interior during the day for warmth at night.

A centrally located "energy tower" holds both an active wind and solar energy system. The wind turbine (which also stores energy in a battery bank system) provides the home's general energy requirements, while the small solar PV is used to heat water. Two large water tanks are used for fire suppression, a common requirement of the Australian outback. All heating and cooling relies on the passive qualities of the home, rather than actively acquired energy. This feature is one of the most unique for contemporary homes, yet completely achievable in such a locale.

If we are to learn only one lesson from the Monier House, it is that

Above, left: A diagram of the section through the Monier house shows the passive strategies for heating and cooling the house.

Above, right: The Monier House centers its alternative energy technologies at a single point, creating a sculptural tower. The home's simple volumes and material palette echo the historical and regional character, minimizing imported materials and using locally found materials.

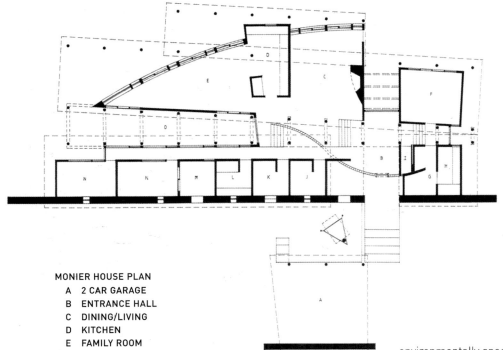

MONIER HOUSE PLAN

A 2 CAR GARAGE
B ENTRANCE HALL
C DINING/LIVING
D KITCHEN
E FAMILY ROOM
F MASTER BEDROOM
G DRESSING ROOM
H ENSUITE
I W.C.
J STUDY
K LAUNDRY
L BATHROOM
M ENCLOSED COURT
N BEDROOM
O COURTYARD
P SOLAR TOWER

environmentally specific designs can and should serve to reduce our overall reliance on active energy for a home. Such a reduction can save the Earth's resources and save money required for energy production that can instead supplement the design budget for the home, consequently enriching our experiences in our living environments.

Center for Maximum Potential Building Systems. Pliny Fisk and Gail Vittorri, American pioneers in environmental sustainability and energy use, completed the home base for the Center for Maximum Potential Building Systems (CMPBS) in 1997. Initially referred to as the Advanced Green Builder Demonstration project, the building has become the hub of operations for Fisk's and Vittorri's experiments. While the center could be used as a house, complete with movable kitchen and working bathroom, it instead operates as the visitor center and headquarters for the center. Funding provided by the US Department of Energy helped the center investigate everything from active energy systems to gray water reuse and potential materials of assembly. While the Monier House safely demonstrates off-the-grid possibilities within the known realm of systems and materials, the center operates on the margins of what is known. The result is a 2,000-square-foot learning lab built from a collage of innovative material studies for the center's team and the visiting public.

Located on the outskirts of Austin, Texas, the center experiences hot, humid summers and humid, cool winters. Rainfall averages thirty-two inches a year, resulting in a landscape that is lush and that can quickly engulf buildings. The material studies, technologies, and overall systems were developed as a holistic strategy for the facility. Over time, observations of the center may lead to valuable understanding of new ways of building and living.

A key feature and core construction technique is the structural system that Fisk devised of steel rebar columns called GreenForms. GreenForms are assembled like an erector set, providing a framework of interior and exterior columns and beams as well as securing points for materials to make walls. The frames are in-filled or clad with a variety of highly insulative (or high-mass) sustainable materials, such as adobe, rammed earth, straw, and recycled polystyrene, for different spaces. Each infilled or clad wall provides the opportunity to test the assemblies. Calcrete, a concrete-like mixture Fisk developed out of a combination of indigenous caliche and Ashcrete (made with fly ash, a by-product of coal burning), is also used in some infill walls. The roof design and material, and the surrounding landscape provide for an innovative cooling strategy. The majority of the house exterior and roofs are clad in corrugated, galvanized metal, which has a long life in a humid environment. The metal roofs are designed to collect rainwater into large cisterns for use by the center's team. Landscaping is used not only to create cool shade in and around the center, but also to aid in the treatment of wastewater generated at the center. The house is passively cooled by natural breezes and a low-tech evaporative cooling system comprised of trickling water over the metal roof at night.

Conventions of form and location associated with bathroom and kitchen are reconsidered from both sustainable and lifestyle expectations. The bathroom in the center is a cleverly designed space that has a single

■

Opposite: The center, with its vibrant collage of materials and forms is a direct expression of the variety of wall assemblies being studied.

Above, left: Fisk's GreenForms, built of steel rebar, provide a simple structural system on which to build.

Above, right: The CMPBS Solar Decathlon Home, complete with traveling trailer labs, which "plugs" into the home to add living space.

drain "pole" with a swiveling shower head and sink that allows a second person to use the bathroom by simply rotating the fixtures around the pole opposing the fixtures. Rather than create a separate shower pan, the floor of the bathroom holds a drain, allowing the water to drain into it regardless of the orientation of the shower head. The kitchen is also an invention inspired by the Texas environment. Rather than create a built-in kitchen that heats up the house in the summer, Fisk designed a series of cabinets on wheels with sink and

stove that are hitched together. The drain system is detailed with a quick release for removing the kitchen "train" from the interior to an outside patio in a matter of minutes. When the heat is too much to sleep through inside, there are elevated exterior sleeping platforms that are cooled by the evening breeze.

The center's design along with the flexible comfort level of its inhabitants allows for a scaled-down system for energy generation. The primary power source is a small array of PV panels that are

supported with a backup generator.

In the past nine years, the original structure has aged and evolved and new experiments for living and working have been added. The award-winning Solar Decathlon Home, an 800-square-foot solar-powered house initially displayed on the Mall in Washington, D.C., now resides adjacent to the original center building, providing an aggregate of knowledge and experience for a team of explorers. The center continues to evolve as systems are explored and different low-impact building materials and methods are tested. Unlike many buildings, the center is an evolving environment, a place designed for change and experiment; it is a true learning lab.

Environmental Showcase Home. In 1992, Mark DeMichele, president and CEO of the Arizona Department of Public Service, decided to develop an Environmental Showcase Home (ESH) for the Southwest to demonstrate sustainable and off-the-grid living for the region. Through research gained from a 1992 focus group of home buyers, the researchers "concluded that members of the public do not normally associate environmental issues with the kinds of homes they buy."[6] With this lack of associated cause and effect, home buyers bring no demands upon builders to modify their construction methods, techniques, energy systems, or materials. With the potential presentation and education of a case study home, however, the public can become more knowledgeable of what is potentially harmful to the environment and themselves with conventional building and design practices and what they may consider to create a more

The Environmental showcase home provides the visiting public with the opportunity to explore multiple strategies and uses of alternative energy, including rainwater collection, gray water reuse, PV energy, and active heating and cooling.

sustainable home. Through an open competition, Eddie Jones of Jones Studio in Phoenix, Arizona, was selected to design the ESH. In January 1995, it was opened to the public.

A primary concern of Jones Studio was how to appropriately respond to the environment and climate, a consideration missing in most houses in the region. As with many homes across the West, the typical Phoenix house is a misplaced California-style home. Large glass openings with minimal overhangs, appropriate and responsive to California's more temperate climate and cool breezes, found their way into the Arizona desert in the 1940s. Perhaps formally inspired by the AA Case Study program itself, but without reconsidering the appropriate architectural response for a distinctly different environment, this building language has resulted in homes that require massive amounts of air-conditioning to combat the heat gain collected through the large glass windows. The misplaced California house type inspired thousands of energy- and resource-hungry homes throughout the expanding cities of the Southwest.

With such lessons in mind and research of the adobe architecture born of this region, Jones Studio embarked on the design for the ESH.

The ESH is designed to incorporate not only new technologies to minimize and conserve energy but also to consider an appropriate architectural response to the climate and environment of the Sonoran Desert. The first design strategy of the ESH is its orientation on the site. To allow for integration of solar conditions, the house was oriented with its long side extending east to west. Its south face creates the enclosure to the living areas with large sliding glass doors that can be modified with solar shading and operable windows. A north-facing clerestory window runs the length of the home, including the living area and kitchen, to not only provide filtered daylight to the center of the house but also a method of natural ventilation in the home.

Out from the glass doors of the living room lies a small swimming pool. Pools are prevalent in the backyards of the Southwest, yet they are a drain on limited resources, especially water. Rather than not include a swimming pool in the home's design,

it was decided that a more resource-conserving pool would provide lessons for an inevitable attribute that most homeowners would incorporate. The pool is heated with solar hot-water heaters located on the roof; its water acts as a fire-suppression reservoir, and the water is filtered by a non-chlorine ionization unit.

A butterfly roof extends over the house and collects rainwater in an underground cistern that provides automatic underground "drip" irrigation for the xeriscape landscape. A second butterfly roof occurs above the garage, which also collects rainwater into an above-ground cistern that can be used to gravity feed the adjacent garden with an attached water hose. Gray water is collected from the sinks and shower in the house and stored in an underground cistern to feed into the underground irrigation system. The roof of the house is angled for optimal solar orientation for the hot-water panels and PV panels, which generate 2.7 kW of electricity (with battery bank). Several high-efficiency heating and cooling units, including one that also produces domestic hot water, are used in the house and garage. Visitors to the house can see the systems for themselves, understand how they work, and consider the monitoring data prior to selecting a particular system for their own home.

The home's materials also provide sustainable qualities of design. The floor of the house is a concrete slab with fly ash mixture. Much of the thermal envelope (exterior walls) of the house are made of exposed, lightweight, insulated concrete masonry blocks, called Integra, which have their hollow centers filled with Supergreen foam insulation for a total R-value of 24. Nature Guard insulation is used for the roof and wood-frame wall insulation. Large south-facing glass doors and lower windows "use a high-performance glazing system made up of 1/8-inch-thick tempered gray-tinted outer pane and a 1/8-inch-thick tempered clear inner pane with a low-emissivity coating."[7] An air space between the two glass panes is filled with Argon gas and low-emission film, called Heat Mirror, to help deflect heat gain through the glass. Several canvas coverings and metal-louvers systems over the exterior spaces adjacent to the home help to shade the house from summer sun and provide shaded spaces for outdoor living.

The additional design techniques and sustainable features are extensive in the ESH—so extensive in fact that a complete book, *The Environment Comes Home*, was written to thoroughly document and explain all the details of the design. The ESH is monitored by Arizona State University in order to provide long-term data from which a better understanding of the efficiency of the active and passive systems of the house can be gained. The ESH demonstrates that not only can a house be designed and built that conserves resources but that it can also ground its users in the cycles of its place, inspiring a lifestyle that is rooted in its landscape and climactic conditions.

WHO WILL TAKE THE LEAD

These recent case study homes are typically the outcome of a combined vision of groups that may include energy consortiums, not-for-profit organizations, municipal energy programs, and think tanks. A homeowner is not the client or driving vision. The funds come from grants and foundations, not an individual mortgage. Though the case study home provides a fantastic learning opportunity for many, for some demonstration is not

enough. For these individuals, waiting for the governments and public officials to mandate change or instigate sweeping environmental controls cannot occur fast enough. Currently, such people actively engage in finding a way to put into practice a life that more closely considers the health of the planet and the well-being of their society and other societies.

The homes presented in the following section provide great inspiration, for they are the committed visions of everyday people who believe in the responsibility to put new ideas into action in order to conserve resources and energy—and protect the planet. They are the mavericks of communities, the leaders we should all thank for providing us with vision of great breadth and potential for a new way of living.

Above: The ESH follows open-plan living similar to the plans from the AA Case Study houses. The incorporation of a clerestory at the center of the house brings in natural light and naturally ventilates the home.

[1] I use the term *modern* in this essay to associate particular cultural beliefs and practices that have evolved out of and are associated with the modern paradigm of thought, the concept of progress, the enlightenment era, and the Cartesian mindset. While this intellectual paradigm developed in the Western world, it is no longer confined to such a limited geographic reference. Therefore, *modern* is employed for its intellectual reference as it expands across the globe to all those cultures who are adopting it.

[2] The writing of some of the cultural leaders of the time, such as Frank Lloyd Wright, Gertrude Stein, Dorothy Parker, Zora Neale Hurston, Robert Sherman, and others, suggest a change in the way people saw themselves in the world in the late 1940s and 1950s. There was a transition in the interpretation of independence and freedom.

[3] Esther McCoy, *Case Study Houses: 1945–1962* (Hennessey + Ingalls, Santa Monica, CA: 1977), 2.

[4] See www.bfi.org.

[5] Ibid.

[6] K. David Pijawka and Kim Shetter, *The Environment Comes Home: Arizona Public Service's Environmental Showcase Home* (The University of Arizona Press, Tempe, AZ: 1995), 5.

[7] Ibid., 38.

Left: A whimsical rain chain hangs from the end of the scupper, which brings rainwater to the cistern.

The projects:
Six in-depth case studies

"Our ideals, laws and customs should be based on the proposition that each generation, in turn, becomes the custodian rather than the absolute owner of our resources and each generation has the obligation to pass this inheritance on to the future."

— Charles A. Lindbergh, New York Times Magazine, May 23, 1971

Bruny Island Guesthouse

Bruny Island, Tasmania, Australia ▪ 1+2 Architecture ▪ 2,150 sq. ft.

The remoteness of the Bruny Island guesthouse cannot be overemphasized. This is not a place from which you can simply come and go. It is a place that requires a commitment for the journey. After the ferry ride from the tiny port town of the mainland in Tasmania, you make a thirty-minute drive across unimproved roads through the eucalyptus and casuarina trees into the outback, as these remote lands are called. The road curves west, arriving at a point of the island called Mickey's Point, with surrounding water on three sides. The point is not only the perfect setting for someone looking for a place to feel like part of the landscape and its immensity, it also provides great environmental qualities for

an energy-efficient home. Lying at the edge of the water in a typically mild climate, the house is sited with its long side stretching east to west in order to take in the sun's rays in winter. The siting also allows the house to be cooled by the predominant westerly winds during the warm season. Entry into the house is from the south, between the bedroom volumes. One enters into an intentionally low-roofed breezeway, which acts as the spine and main circulation through the home, and into the living space,

which extends up and out toward the water through the curved ceiling. The spatial sequence of the home plays into the visitor's anticipation that has grown during the long trip across the water and onto the island. The dramatic spatial release of the living area extends the visitor's sense of arrival, bringing an intense experience of the place.

The experiential and passive energy strategy is interwoven into the guesthouse's design. The low-roofed spine that separates two linear volumes is

Above: The large glass openings not only provide stunning views to the water, they also allow solar heat into the house in winter and ventilation in summer.

Opposite, left: The entry "breezeway" acts as the circulation spine through the home, and an intimate scaled space that opens into the open living space.

Opposite, right: Dining, living, and kitchen areas are all shared in one central space, which opens out to the water beyond. These shared spaces can minimize the overall size of a house and help to conserve energy.

oriented east to west, allowing for a maximized exposure toward the water and winter solar gain. The larger volume fronts the water, with a master bedroom suite at one end and public space on the other providing for relaxation, entertaining, and cooking. It is heated and cooled passively through the large, operable window, wall, and doors onto the west porch. The smaller entry volume sits behind with a guest suite and children's bedroom. The roofs for both living and sleeping volumes echo each other through the dynamic use of a reverse curve extending out to create overhangs. The deep overhangs serve multiple purposes. Not only do they act as solar shading from the summer sun and provide large, covered porches, they also allow the sunlight to refract back into the interior without creating harsh shadows that can occur from flat surfaces and overhangs. Additional solar shading is provided by thin, horizontal "fins" that extend perpendicularly from the glass wall, allowing winter sun in and

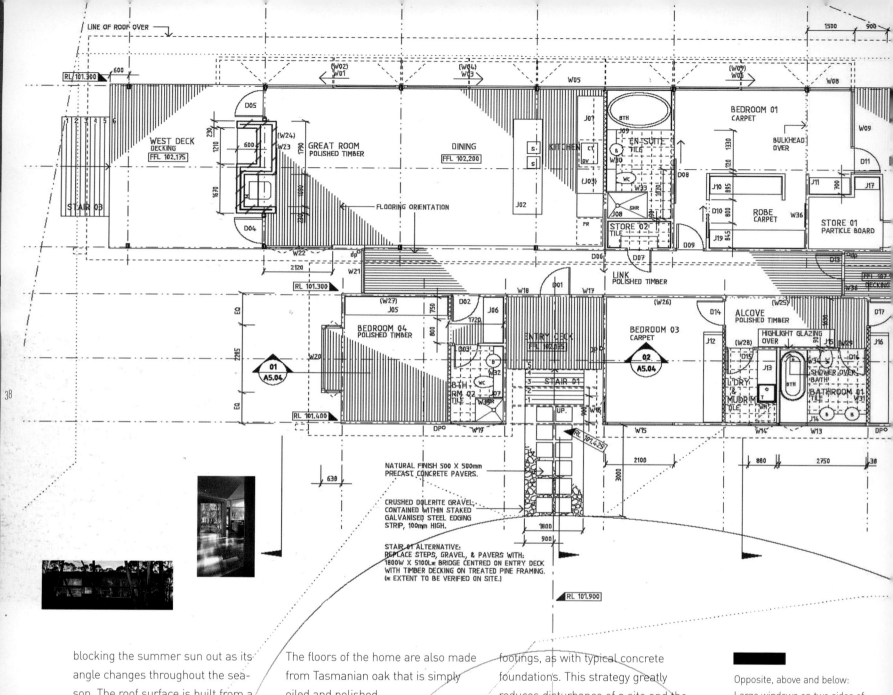

Floor plan labels (as annotated on drawing):

LINE OF ROOF OVER

RL 101.300

WEST DECK
DECKING
FFL 102.175

STAIR 03

GREAT ROOM
POLISHED TIMBER

DINING
FFL 102.200

FLOORING ORIENTATION

KITCHEN

BTH

EN-SUITE
TILE

BEDROOM 01
CARPET

BULKHEAD OVER

WC

SHR

STORE 02
TILE

ROBE
CARPET

STORE 01
PARTICLE BOARD

LINK
POLISHED TIMBER

BEDROOM 04
POLISHED TIMBER

ENTRY DECK
FFL 102.025

BEDROOM 03
CARPET

ALCOVE
POLISHED TIMBER

HIGHLIGHT GLAZING OVER

01
A5.04

02
A5.04

BTH RM 02
TILE

WC

STAIR 01

L'DRY &
MUDRM
TILE

SHOWER OVER
BATH

BATHROOM 01
TILE

RL 101.300

RL 101.400

RL 101.425

NATURAL FINISH 500 X 500mm
PRECAST CONCRETE PAVERS.

CRUSHED DOLERITE GRAVEL,
CONTAINED WITHIN STAKED
GALVANISED STEEL EDGING
STRIP, 100mm HIGH.

STAIR 01 ALTERNATIVE:
REPLACE STEPS, GRAVEL, & PAVERS WITH:
1800W X 5100L± BRIDGE CENTRED ON ENTRY DECK
WITH TIMBER DECKING ON TREATED PINE FRAMING.
(± EXTENT TO BE VERIFIED ON SITE.)

RL 101.900

---

blocking the summer sun out as its angle changes throughout the season. The roof surface is built from a low-profile corrugated metal, which is perforated at its edge to allow water to pass into the gutter below while minimizing the debris that collects in the gutter. Low-maintenance and fire-resistant Galvalume cladding is used on the exterior walls along with sustainable, oiled Tasmanian oak, a eucalyptus species from Australia.

The floors of the home are also made from Tasmanian oak that is simply oiled and polished.

The sensitivity to the place, as demonstrated in the arrival sequence, carries through the many considerations for the retreat, from construction and materials to the incorporation of the energy system. The house lightly touches the ground with steel feet on concrete pilings, dispensing with the need for continuous concrete

footings, as with typical concrete foundations. This strategy greatly reduces disturbance of a site and the requirement to remove massive amounts of earth for a concrete-foundation-wall system.

In addition to the passive heating and cooling, other energy-efficient strategies were considered in both design and material assembly. A key to minimizing the overall energy requirement was the incorporation of

Opposite, above and below:
Large windows on two sides of the living area dissolve the visual separation between interior and exterior. A low-profile fireplace reduces its visual impact on the room while providing heat.

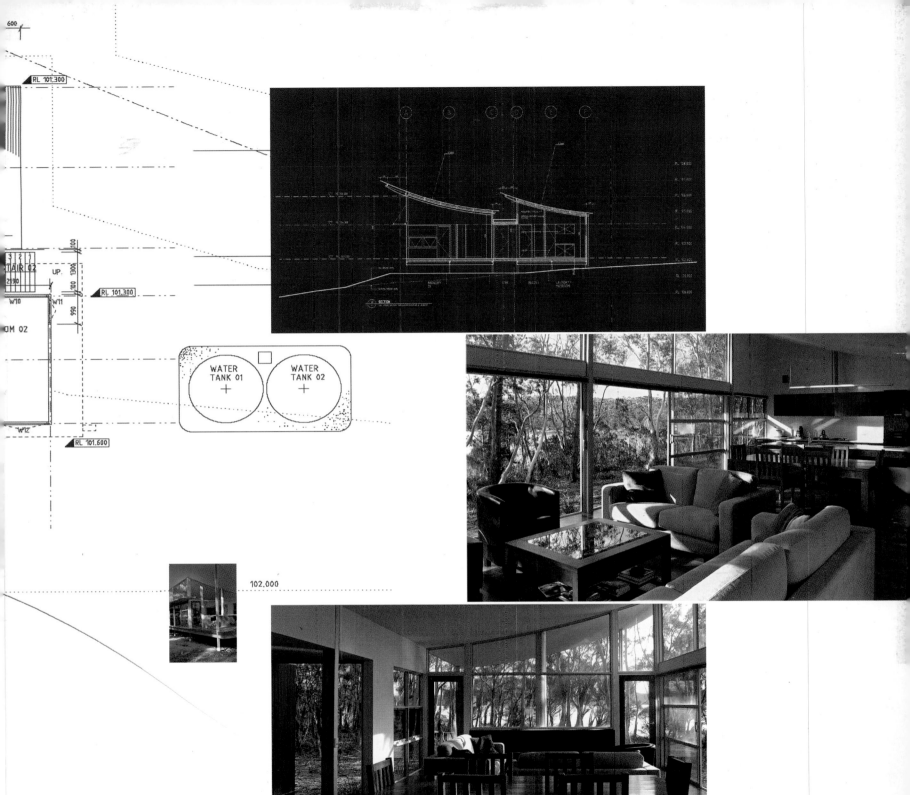

RL 101.300

STAIR 02

UP.

W10   W11

OM 02

RL 101.300

W12

RL 101.600

WATER
TANK 01
+

WATER
TANK 02
+

102.000

Water Collection and Gray Water Reuse Systems

Rainwater collection is a simple, low-tech, low-cost first step that can be taken to help conserve resources.

Irrigating the Landscape

Rainwater collected from a roof can be stored in a variety of ways, or at the very least redirected to water a particular aspect of the landscape. The landscape you plant directly affects the amount of rainwater you need to collect. If you live in an arid environment and have a full green lawn with tropical plants, you probably will never collect enough rainwater over the year to water your vegetation. If you want to live a less-resource-reliant existence, you should change your landscape strategy and incorporate plants that can survive with minimal irrigation.

Cisterns and Barrels

The size of the collection device is determined by the amount of rain you receive, when you receive it, the amount you want to collect and store, and what you want to achieve with the collected water.

If you live in an area that receives periodic or frequent rain and wish to only water a specific, small section of a garden, you could store your water in rain barrels from the gutter and use gravity to feed the water into a hose for watering.

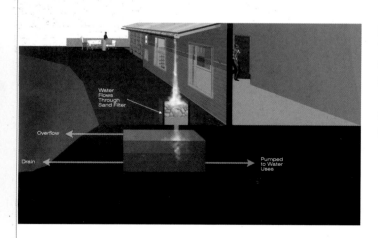

If you live in the Seattle or Oregon, for instance, where it rains frequently, you may only need rainwater to irrigate in the few dry months of the summer. With intermittent rain during the summer, you would only collect and store a small amount to be dispersed during these months.

However, if you live an arid environment, such as Arizona, New Mexico, or Tasmania with a low-water-use landscape (also called xeriscape), you could store the majority of the rainwater that occurs in the few months of the year and use it to irrigate throughout the year. This would require a

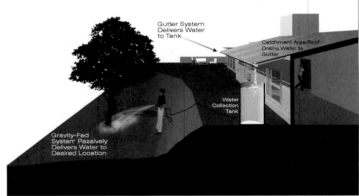

large cistern, most likely located underground or in a crawl space with a pump and simple filtration system to keep the water free of debris and insects.

Rainwater can also be collected in a cistern and used not only for irrigation but also for flushing water in toilets. This dual system uses water that is perfectly safe and appropriate for such water use, reducing the overall stress placed on the environment and its resources. Such a system is planned for the Capitol Hill House profiled on pages 46–59. In the Bruny Island guesthouse, rainwater collected in a cistern provides all domestic water.

Gray Water Collection and Reuse

Gray water is used domestic water from showers and bathroom sinks that typically goes into our sewers or septic systems. This "used" water can be collected in some municipalities for reuse in landscape irrigation or toilets. If you are in such a municipality, gray water is typically stored in a cistern and designed to be released into the landscape through an underground irrigation system. This method does not allow human contact with the water and is believed to be the safest application of the reuse of gray water.

█████

A single roof plane extends from interior ceiling to overhang and porches, unifying the home's expression inside and out. Metal horizontal fins help to block summer sun from entering the house.

well-insulated walls with rock wool common to Australia, a healthy and sustainable insulation that is a composite derived from sheep's wool. Organizing the design through two linear volumes allows for the separation of the primary living area and master suite from the guest's and children's rooms and creates the ability to close parts of the house that are not in use, maximizing the solar or thermal heat collected and generated. Retaining the house at a single story not only minimizes the profile of the house on the landscape but also allows the heating to occur primarily through passive solar collection supplemented by a low-profile fireplace in the main living area and secondary heating units in each bedroom. Forgoing a central heating system minimizes overall energy use. Cross ventilation through both volumes is created through a series of operable clerestories above the circulation spine.

The guesthouse exists fully independent from the municipal grid. Active energy is gained through a three-layered strategy. A PV solar array is located atop a salvaged shipping container, which also houses all of the mechanical requirements, including the battery bank, inverter, and backup generator. The solar array accounts for the retreat's general domestic power use. Gas tanks, which can be refilled, are used for heating water and small heating units for each of the bedrooms. Two 2,600-gallon underground tanks store rainwater collected from the roofs. Water is then pumped up into the house for the various domestic uses, including the spa-size tub in the master bath, one of the splurges for the retreat.

Due to the intermittent use of the retreat, a conventional septic system was not an option. Waste from the house is managed through a black-water collection point and gray-water reclamation system. This system

Bruny Island GUESTHOUSE Strategies

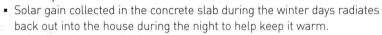

Materials

- The material palette is kept to a minimum to offset costs incurred by shipping multiple materials to a remote site.
- Additional cost and energy savings are gained by on-site steel fabrication and welding.
- Sustainable Tasmanian oak, a eucalyptus species from Australia with an oil finish, is used on the exterior walls as well as interior floors.
- Low-maintenance and fire-resistant Galvalume cladding is used on the exterior walls.
- Insulation is recycled polyester/wool insulation (rock wool), a sustainable and locally fabricated product readily available in Australia.

Passive Techniques

- Solar gain collected in the concrete slab during the winter days radiates back out into the house during the night to help keep it warm.
- Operable windows from front to back provide for passive cooling throughout the house during the summer.
- Roof overhangs shade the house from summer sun.

Active Technologies

- A 960-kW PV BP fixed-mount array (6 panels x 160 W) provides almost 100 percent of electrical requirements (additional load is provided by a backup generator).
- Exide battery bank, 24 V, with a capacity of 830 Ah.
- Latronics inverter, with output of 3,000 W (surge output of 9,000 W), transforms the solar energy from dc power to ac power for domestic use.
- Backup gas generator for electrical loads.
- Gas system supplied by tanks for heating and hot water.
- Gray water reclamation through trenches that provide additional moisture to encourage landscape growth.
- Rainwater collection in two 2,600-gallon tanks that are pumped by solar power into house for domestic use.

Rainwater collected off the galvanized, corrugated metal surface is collected into covered gutters and then into two 2,600 gallon underground tanks for all domestic water use.

allows the release of gray water into trenches after passing through a series of "treatment" steps. The release of the gray water can be used to encourage plant growth in the vicinity of the release area and is completely benign to the environment.

The Bruny Island Guesthouse is a rich example of what can be achieved with minimal architectural gestures, minimal material palette, a conscientious concern for budget, and a commitment to sustainability. For its occupants, the guesthouse creates ties to Mickey's Point, not only through the home's design-sensitive interpretation of the place, but also through the integration of the various passive strategies, which require human participation to activate the environmental interface of the house.

Capitol Hill House

Seattle, Washington ▪ BLIP design ▪ 4,200 sq. ft.

W

When people are looking to invest in a home, a common question is whether to buy new, commission and build a home, or buy an older existing home and remodel. In many large cities, if you would like to live in town, buying an older existing home is a common choice. If you are interested in living a more sustainable lifestyle, the purchase of an existing home in a metropolitan area can make a lot of sense. Public transportation, shorter traveling distances to work and community activities, existing utilities, and infrastructure can all reduce the overall resources required for day-to-day living. Remodeling an existing home most often requires less resources and energy than constructing a building from the ground up.

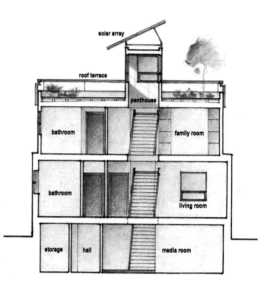

solar array

roof terrace

penthouse

bathroom

family room

bathroom

living room

storage   hall   media room

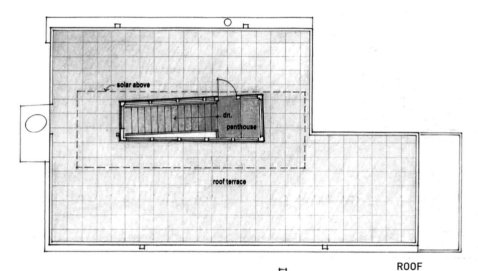

solar above

dn.

penthouse

roof terrace

ROOF

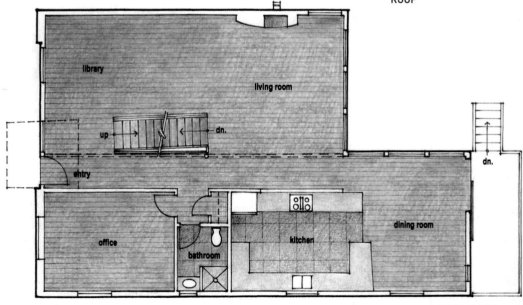

library

living room

up   dn.

dn.

entry

office

bathroom

kitchen

dining room

MAIN FLOOR

It was this line of thinking that led Jo and Ophir Salant-Ronen to buy an existing home in the Capitol Hill area of Seattle, with the intent of remodeling and turning it into a "showcase" of sustainability for other homeowners to learn from. From the architect's point of view, the option for a remodel also offered the opportunity to bring the house into better proportion, character, and sensibility with its surroundings, while also integrating

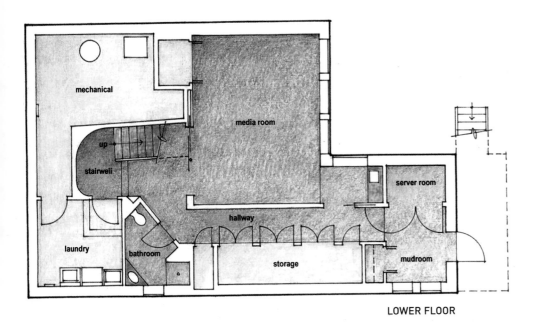

LOWER FLOOR

sustainable materials and technologies. Through the reworking of the home's exterior, it has become a dynamic cultural contribution to the surrounding neighborhood, not only in terms of the visibility of its alternative technologies but also in terms of pushing the perceptions of how modern architecture can belong to an older community of houses.

An initial design decision for the interior was to open the home to create more public space for the growing family of three. Opening up the interior space also capitalized on the great views across the surrounding hills and toward the bay. The entry level of the home now offers an expansive public space, which includes the living, library, dining, and kitchen areas, along with exterior balcony at the back of the house. The original closed condition of the home was also transformed through the redesign of the stair system. The open risers and minimal handrail profile allow the stair system to contribute to the openness of the home. From top to bottom, great natural lighting enters the home, washing down the walls and through the open staircase to the floors below, while allowing hot air to exhaust at the top. Additional public space reached through the stair tower was gained with a rooftop terrace with stunning views of surrounding Seattle.

Left: Bamboo, a rapid re-growth plant, is used on the main living floor. Open riser stair trends of reclaimed Douglas fir help to open the home from floor to floor.

Above: The stair to the rooftop terrace has a window seat at the landing, which provides a great place to view the city in inclement weather. The glass "tower" at the rooftop allows light to wash down the stair core to the floors below.

Above, right: The kitchen opens onto the living space, gaining great views to the water and natural light. Paperstone, a recycled paper product is used for the kitchen counters.

Right: In the living room, large windows with operable components allow for passive cooling and ventilation through the house as well as great views to the water.

Opposite: Large sliding doors open onto balconies built of IPE, a FSC-certified lumber from South America, which has qualities similar to teak.

The optimal location for the PV system and solar hot-water collectors was created on the rooftop of the stair gallery. At night, the stair tower glows like a lantern, creating a dynamic event for those outside. Thoughtful details, such as the window seat at the top of the stairs, help make the rooftop a wonderful place to be, even in inclement weather. Between the entry level and the roof terrace are three bedrooms, two bathrooms, and a large family room, all located on the second level. A large entertainment room is located in the basement along with support spaces and access out to the garage and backyard.

As the house was conceived as a "showcase" for sustainable living, sustainable materials for construction were also incorporated. These materials are readily available for anyone to incorporate into their home and can help reduce the stress we put on the planet. Many of the materials come from a by-product of an existing process or material or may be of a recycled material. Their means of manufacture, method of harvesting, or ability to be quickly replenished can also result in the sustainable condition of a particular material. The original basement floor was replaced with a fly ash concrete

slab with radiant heat, creating the opportunity to increase the original floor-to-ceiling height. Flooring at the main and second level is bamboo with reclaimed fir treads on the stair. Sustainably harvested Ipe is used for the exterior wood decking. Marmoleum is installed on the kitchen and bathroom floors, providing an easy-to-clean surface that adds additional color to the interior. Paperstone, a recycled-paper-content solid surface, is used on the counters in the kitchen.

By far, the most dynamic features of the sustainable attributes of the house are the PV and solar hot-water systems, which contribute to the greatest long-term resource conservation in the house. Despite what one may imagine of Seattle, with its three-hundred-plus days of overcast skies in a year, the solar intake is extraordinary. The PV system is set up as a net-metering system integrated into Seattle's municipal supply that allows the house to receive all the energy it requires while sending extra energy back into the grid. This program allows for the fluctuation of energy production without employing a secondary system to account for additional energy requirements. For instance, during the sunny summer days, the system can provide 100-plus

Photovoltaic Systems

Photovoltaic (PV) systems harvest the energy from the sun in solar collectors. The energy is then transferred from dc into ac electricity through an inverter for domestic use.

The active and most visible component of these systems is the flat panel (called an array), which is ganged together to provide the amount of power you elect to collect or require. The panels can be mounted in ways that optimize collection or minimize the initial expense of the installation.

Mounting Locations (On the Building or Freestanding)

There are three mounting options for PV systems: fixed, single-axis adjustable, and dual-axis adjustable. The fixed system is the most common and most affordable. The panel system is oriented toward the sun typically at the angle of latitude relevant to the residence. In some instances, the fixed angle may be adjusted by the installer in consideration of the tilt of the earth during a particular time of the year. These types of adjustments are typically made to maximize the solar gain and may also be selected if your system is off the grid or a grid intertie.

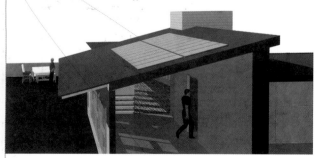

Fixed PV Array

If you live off the grid, in a location that is cold (shorter days in winter) for the majority of the months of the year, you may choose to orient your panels at an angle that more advantageously takes in the winter sun rays to maximize your solar-energy production during the months when you need the energy the most. On the other hand, if your system is a grid intertie and you gain credit for "turning back the meter" that you can use later, you may want to orient your panels to gain the greatest solar collection in the summer when the days are longest.

Most installers believe there are minimal advantages to such small changes in the angle or the array in a single-axis fixed system and prefer to install your PV system at the angle that gives you the greatest overall average of energy collection throughout the year.

If your PV system will be installed on your roof, and your roof is not pitched at the angle of latitude for your locale, you should have your installer verify the efficiency of the angle of your roof. While you will save money installing the fixed system directly to the roof, you may lose money in the long run, and a freestanding fixed system may pay for itself sooner than you think.

Single- and Dual-Axis Systems. The single-axis system is used on freestanding arrays. This system allows you to adjust the panel orientation to the sun's orientation as the earth tilts through the seasons to provide greater solar collection from winter to summer.

A dual-axis system allows an array to not only adjust to the solar orientation according to the season but also follow the sun from sunrise to sunset. These systems are not adjusted by hand but have a mechanical pivot that provides for the tracking of the sun.

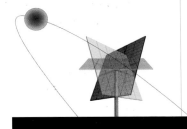

Dual-Axis System

A PV tracking system can work in one of two ways. In the mechanical tracking system, the adjustable mount is connected to a computer with a sensor that gauges the location of the sun. In the passive system, the tracking occurs non-mechanically, through a drum containing oil that is mounted to the pivot location. As the sun heats up the oil, the oil expands and shifts the weight within the drum, consequently shifting the panel. This shifting (and tracking) occurs throughout the day following the sun relative to the heat in the drum. These systems provide the optimal solar orientation for optimal solar intake but cost more than the fixed array or the freestanding single-axis pivot array.

Single-Axis System

Integrating PV Systems for Domestic Use

Grid Intertie. A PV system used in conjunction with the municipal grid system can provide a great advantage to the homeowner. If you have the option, or are required to be tied to the municipal system, and the municipal system offers a buyback or credit program, the grid tie can act as your battery bank. This means that when you are

collecting more solar power than you are using (say, during the longer days of summer), you can generate a credit (long-term storage, like a battery bank). This credit is later returned to you through the municipal system during the shorter days of winter, or during overcast days when you are not generating as much solar power, yet you require power.

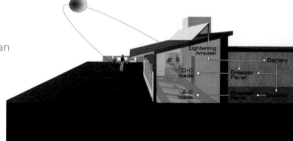

PV Fully Off the Grid

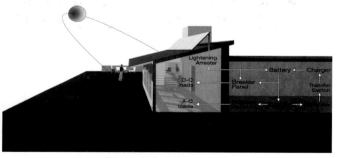

PV-Hybrid Fully Off the Grid

If your municipal grid system does not offer a buyback program, you could install a small battery bank while remaining tied to the grid. This system allows you to store a small amount of energy for high-demand nights or short demands (such as an overcast day) without first tapping into the municipal system. This battery bank allows you to seamlessly connect into the municipal system as a last resort.

Alternative Energy Installations and Support

Inverters. Inverters are required of all alternative-energy collectors, including PV arrays, wind turbines, and hydro power. An inverter translates the power generated from dc to ac, which is the common power current that appliances and systems require. The inverter is placed in line with, but prior to, the breaker panel in the home.

Battery Banks. Battery banks are incorporated into alternative-energy systems to store additional energy generated by the alternative-power systems. Their size is dependent on the goals for their use. Battery banks, like a car battery, have a limited life and must be replaced periodically. The batteries cannot be refurbished and, to date, add to our landfills. For this reason, many homeowners choose to use the municipal grid as their storage method.

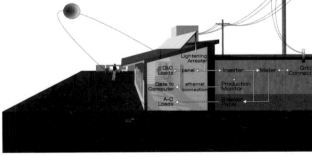

PV-Grid Intertie

Backup Generators. In mild climates, which have consistent weather for solar collection, a homeowner could live off the grid with only PV power for power generation and a small battery bank and a back-up generator. The concept of the backup generator is that it is seldom used; it is available for use in the case of a storm or failure of the alternative-power source or battery bank.

The
Smart
House system
helps to
reduce the
overall energy
use of the
home well
below
the typical
small family
house.

beyond their own ability to produce energy, the Salant-Ronens have the ability to measure their energy use against their overall energy production throughout the year.

A future system for the house, which has already been accounted for in the home's design and infrastructure, is a water-collection tank. The roof deck is finished with a membrane and topped with concrete pavers that will allow rainwater to drain down the walls, into scuppers, and then into the tank. When the Salant-Ronens are ready, they will install a 12,000-gallon cistern in the gravel driveway of the home. The reclaimed water will be used for flushing toilets and irrigating the landscape.

The Capitol Hill House is a great example of remodeling an in-town home to save energy and live a more sustainable life. While the size of the house is large by most standards today, the Smart House system, which is avidly observed, helps to reduce the overall energy use of the home well below the typical small family house.

Opposite: The PV array and solar hot-water heater are simply mounted to a steel substructure angled for optimum solar collection.

Above: Seen from the street, the PV array and solar hot-water panels provide a reminder to the community of the need to conserve energy. They also bring a new sculptural element to the neighborhood skyline.

percent of the amount of energy required for the house, resulting in a credit that can be used for overcast days in the year. During overcast weather, the house can draw as much energy as it needs from the grid-tie, which acts as a "battery bank" for the home. On average, the system produces 3,200 kWh/year, almost 100 percent of the energy the home requires.

One of the successes to this system is the Smart House technology, which allows the owners to monitor the energy use of the home, modify their energy use, and, consequently, adjust their overall energy requirements. These modifications have led to a reduction in the amount of the supplemental heat required of the boiler, as well as knowledge of how much energy appliances use, when they may be used most efficiently, and when energy is most abundant. Regardless of the option of "endless" energy from the municipal grid,

Strategies

Passive Techniques

- Operable windows from front to back of the house and a passive solar chimney at the top of the stairs to the roof patio allow for passive cooling through the house.
- The house is well insulated and thus air-tight, which makes it highly efficient in terms of heating and cooling. The air tightness of the house is complemented by a whole-house intake-and-ventilation system that provides the appropriate amount of fresh-air exchange.

Active Technologies

- A 3,060-kW BP PV system (18 panels x 170 W) provides almost 100 percent of the electrical requirements for the home. It is installed as a grid intertie system.
- Two 30-tube evacuated-tube solar hot-water collectors by Thermomax reduce the overall energy required to generate domestic hot water. All domestic water is also heated first with the Thermomax solar hot-water system, and supplemented by the gas boiler.
- SMA Sunny Boy 2,500 W/240 V inverter transforms the solar energy from dc power to ac power for domestic use.
- A small battery backup system is installed in the instance of power failures.
- Wastewater Heat Recovery system, a highly efficient system, which employs GFX (Gravity-Film Heat Exchange) technology to transfer heat gained from the warm "gray water" running down the copper drain pipe to the

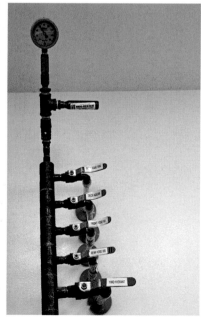

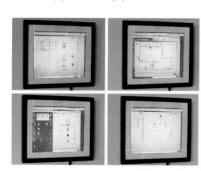

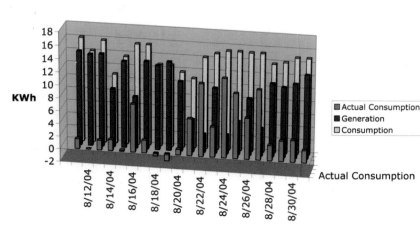

August

KWh

Legend:
- Actual Consumption
- Generation
- Consumption

X-axis: 8/12/04, 8/14/04, 8/16/04, 8/18/04, 8/20/04, 8/22/04, 8/24/04, 8/26/04, 8/28/04, 8/30/04

Y-axis: -2, 0, 2, 4, 6, 8, 10, 12, 14, 16, 18

Actual Consumption

Materials

incoming supply, which is wrapped around the drain pipe, to preheat the water for the shower.

- Radiant-heat in-floor system installed in a concrete topping slab is primarily heated by the solar hot-water system and supplemented by a Viessman high-efficiency gas boiler.
- A Smart House technology system is tied to the computer to monitor the home's energy use, allowing the owner to both understand their energy-use patterns and modify the way they use energy to create a more sustainable lifestyle. Smart House technology could also be added post construction using the existing line voltage wiring for communication.
- Motion detectors installed in rooms are used to both turn off lights in a vacant room and turn on the boiler system for a short amount of time when someone enters the bathroom.
- The house is plumbed for a future 12,000-gallon rainwater collection tank to be installed under the gravel driveway to provide water for toilet flushing and landscape irrigation.

- Insulation in the walls and ceiling is Icynene, an open-cell system that is bio-degradable and has minimal off-gassing.
- Rain-screen siding, a system off-set from the enclosure surface of the house, is used to minimize the moisture in the wall cavity, reduce heat gain at the wall surface, and allow for evaporation of trapped moisture.
- Low-voltage and fluorescent lighting, which have reduced energy requirements, are used throughout.
- All appliances are Energy Star rated for their efficiency for energy and other resources.
- Low-water-use plumbing fixtures are in use.
- Low- or no-VOC paint provides the finish surface on the interior walls.
- Bamboo and recycled Douglas fir are used for flooring and stair treads.
- Ipe, a sustainable, harvested, long-lasting wood from South America, is used for exterior decking.

59

Outside/In House and Studio

Livingston, Montana ▪ Ryker/Nave Design ▪ House: 2,200 sq. ft. ▪ Studio: 1,600 sq. ft.

M

Montana is large, expansive, and dramatic. The land can be felt as a sculpture through which people move. The Outside/In House and Studio is conceived as a response to the landscape in which it is situated. Located in the rural landscape just outside of Livingston, Montana, the house has views of the nearby Absaroka-Beartooth Wilderness and Absaroka Mountains to the east and the foothills of the Gallatin Mountain Range to the West. Rather than stand in contrast to the arid grassland of the site, the buildings lie in repose. Situated between the folds of the hills, they appear and disappear, as one moves across the land. The house steps down the natural slope of the land from east to west through a cascading series of internal spaces.

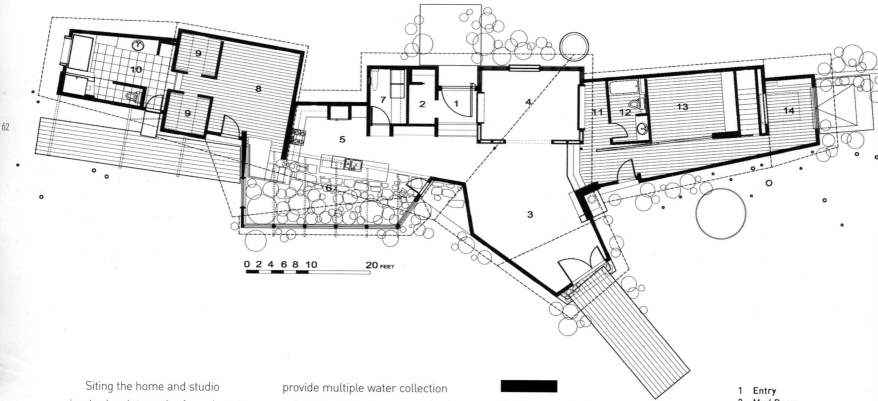

0 2 4 6 8 10   20 FEET

Siting the home and studio involved an integrative formal strategy. The house is situated at the low point of the undulating hills, which minimizes the visual impact of the home on the landscape, blocks the winter winds from the north, and provides a striking view of the mountains. The roofs, which echo the hills, provide multiple water collection points at which above-ground galvanized cisterns are placed to collect rainwater and snow melt for irrigation of the garden areas. Water runoff from overflowing cisterns during the spring also creates a different vegetative condition than the rest of the surrounding, predominately dry

Previous page: The long side of the home is oriented to the south, allowing the sun to passively heat the house in cool weather and southerly breezes to cool the house in summer.

Opposite: The roof profile of the house takes its cue from the surrounding hills and mountains.

1 Entry
2 Mud Room
3 Living Room
4 Dining Room
5 Kitchen
6 Greenhouse
7 Utility Room
8 Bedroom
9 Closet
10 Bath
11 Library
12 Guest Bath
13 Guest Bedroom
14 Study

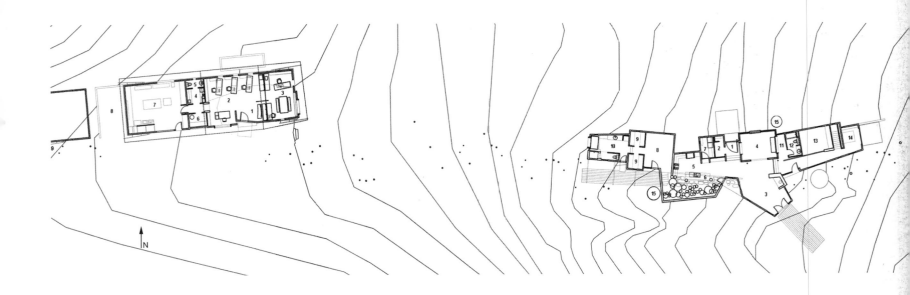

HOUSE
1 Entry
2 Mudroom
3 Living Room
4 Dining Room
5 Kitchen
6 Greenhouse
7 Utility Room
8 Bedroom
9 Closet
10 Bath
11 Library
12 Guest Bath
13 Guest Bedroom
14 Study
15 Water Collection

STUDIO
1 Entry
2 Studio
3 Conference/Office
4 Kitchen
5 Restroom
6 Mechanical/Storage
7 Furniture/Model Shop
8 Equipment Storage
9 Photovoltaic Panels

grassland. From within these different conditions more water-intensive indigenous plants can be grown. Gray water is collected from both of the bathroom sinks, tubs, and showers into two tanks located in the crawl space below the house. A small pump is submerged in each tank with a hose bib to the outside of the house that provides water to irrigate the surrounding garden and grasses. One of the gray-water release zones is specifically graded to concentrate the water along a drainage point to develop a garden that has more of a riparian quality. In the winter, the tanks can be turned off to allow the water to drain directly into the septic system.

Strong sun in winter and summer provides an optimal environment for incorporating passive heating and cooling strategies for both buildings. The long sides of the buildings face south in order to capture both the winter sun and summer southerly breezes. The thin depth of the house and studio from north to south provides for simple ventilation of the low humidity of 90-plus-degree days through the summer months. The

Above, left: Folds in the roof provide for water collection points. Cisterns located below the roof valleys collect water and snow for watering the indigenous plants.

Above, right: A long, narrow deck extends from the living room over the natural grasses. When the wind blows, the feeling is reminiscent of a dock extending over water.

Above: The house follows the slope of the land, dropping nine feet from one end to the other, helping to blend the buildings into the landscape and extend the feeling of the land to the inside.

passive cooling strategy is activated through large operable windows along the south, shaded by deep overhangs that exhaust through windows on the north facade. Ceiling fans in the primary spaces provide adequate air movement in the summer and help to keep the interior cool. The north facades of the home and studio have smaller operable windows to minimize arctic winter winds while allowing ventilation. The concrete slabs of the buildings remain cool in the summer when the angle of the sun is high in the sky.

In the winter, passive solar heating is gained through the southern windows when the sun lies lower in the sky. Solar heat is collected in the concrete slab floors during the day radiating back through the house in the evening. On cool, sunny days, the house is fully heated by the sun, minimizing the mechanical heating requirements. Additional solar heat is taken advantage of with the greenhouse space that is part of the kitchen, connecting the living area to the master bedroom.

The greenhouse space creates a

This page: The kitchen, with greenhouse space, allows the owners to harvest vegetables and herbs all year.

Opposite: The master bedroom stair landing is level with the kitchen counters, creating a visual flow through the space and emphasizing the vertical movement through the house.

large passive solar collection point and a full-year garden. The greenhouse is filled with citrus trees, tomato plants, various herbs, and other ornamental plants that provide humidity to the home in an otherwise extremely arid environment. The greenhouse also creates its own micro climate, moderating the heating and cooling of the home as the garden matures. The greenhouse roof collects water through a butterfly form and is built with a custom steel frame clad in polycarbonate. The polycarbonate provides greater insulation than typical glass systems and decreases the solar gain through the roof as the sun passes over it in the summer. Fabric scrims are hung across the inside of the greenhouse ceiling in summer, providing additional protection from the strong afternoon summer sun in July and August.

The undulating landscape in which the house is sited also initiated the design concept for flowing interior spaces. One enters the interior at the center of the home through a common public space, which holds kitchen, formal dining, living room, and greenhouse. At either end are bedrooms. The master bedroom is

The undulating landscape in which the house is sited initiated the design concept for flowing interior spaces.

located up a series of steps at one end of the greenhouse, the spatial sequence of the bedroom suite ends at the bathroom with views to the west. The guest bedroom wing contains a bedroom, a full guest bath, and a second easterly oriented room, which can be used as an auxiliary guest room when the Murphy bed is folded down. The house has a high degree of openness and flexibility, which not only provides great ventilation, but also allows for future reconsideration of the home's interior use.

Many of the secondary volumes are enclosed at a lower height from the whole volume of the house, creating an inner landscape with contrasting qualities of enclosure and exposure. The tops of these volumes, including the mudroom, laundry, and guest bath, have finished floors to provide lofts for getaway spaces and additional sleeping areas.

While Montana has long winters, it is a place that can be enjoyed throughout the year. For this reason, an emphasis on the ability to move

from inside to outside was incorporated in the design of the house, with doors and decks or raised gardens located adjacent to all of the primary spaces. A future roof deck is planned above the master bathroom to provide views of sunsets and an exterior sleeping space so one can stay cool during the heat of summer.

A minimal material palette helps to reinforce a continuity of experience from space to space. Douglas fir, a wood species local to Montana and the Northwest, is used throughout

Opposite: The master bedroom has a split view to the outside from the greenhouse and directly to the outside.

Left: Concrete floors with radiant heat also absorb sun in the winter for passive heating. The dining room framed wall, made of select cut Douglas fir, is open on the inside and detailed with glass between the outside wall, creating a garden-like space in which to eat.

Above: The circulation through the house moves and adjusts according to different spaces, resulting in a sense of being on a path in the landscape.

Wind Turbine Systems

Many people interested in alternative energy believe that wind turbines have yet to be developed to their highest potential. Others believe that wind turbines are destined to dominate the municipal alternative-energy market. Over the next several years, these beliefs will be challenged and revised as wind energy and its instruments of energy generation evolve. While we are accustomed to seeing the turbines that look similar to the windmills of the Old West, with propellers that turn facing into the wind, new models are being developed. Companies are exploring small modular turbines in series on top of buildings; others are developing turbines that turn horizontally on a vertical axis, appearing more like wind sculpture than energy generator.

Effective Energy Generated by Wind Turbines

The typical wind turbines employed for domestic use have made great strides in efficiency over the past several years. The greatest change has been their ability to remain productive and efficient in greater speeds of wind, with minimized mechanical adjustments and servicing. Today, the typical domestic wind turbine is productive at wind speeds starting at 7 mph (referred to as a cut-in speed), while they are rated for productivity with wind speeds up to 25–35 mph (depending on the manufacturer). The typical speed at which they turn out of the

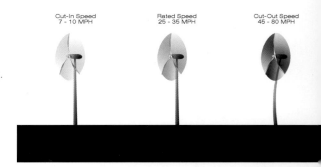

wind, called the cut-out speed, is 45–80 mph. The cut-out attribute is engineered into the turbine, so that it shuts down in high winds to preserve its mechanical integrity.

Another intriguing fact of wind energy when compared to PV power is that PV power systems can only generate a specific rate of power (more sun in the sky still generates the same rate of power), whereas wind generates power at an exponential degree with increased speed of the turbine.

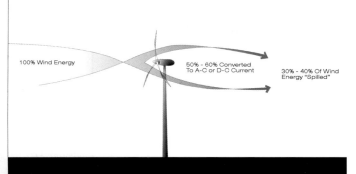

Wind Turbines in a Hybrid System

Wind turbines are not typically the first alternative-energy system adopted, unless you live in an environment with constant and optimal wind conditions. In general, they are used in a hybrid system with PV arrays. The hybrid is used in off-the-grid installations that are located in severe climates, where a battery system cannot feasibly store the amount of energy required to sustain a home through the length of a severe weather disturbance. The conceptual consideration of the hybrid system is that if it is sunny you don't need it or there may not be strong winds in your area. Yet, if it is stormy, and there is no sun, the wind will be blowing and you can generate your energy with a wind turbine.

In places of extreme environmental conditions, where the weather can have long periods of overcast skies, extreme cold, or large power loads, for domestic use such as forced-air cooling, a home would require more energy than you could store in a battery bank. In these instances, a hybrid system makes sense and may be required. If you live in a milder climate, a hybrid may not be necessary because strong weather storms are short lived and your battery bank can sustain you through these periods.

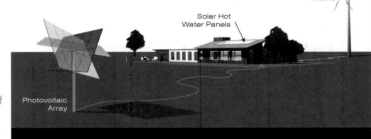

A Fully Off-the-Grid System

Backup Generators. Additionally, a generator can also be included in a hybrid system. While generators are gas driven, some homeowners are making their generators more sustainable by using diesel generators that can operate with biodiesel rather than straight diesel.

Backup Generators in a Hybrid System. Lastly, extreme climatic locales should also incorporate a backup generator. These, of course, are the method of last resort when used with a hybrid system, such as PVs combined with a wind turbine. But if you are living off the gird and your wind turbine fails during a 25-below-zero snowstorm, which lasts five days, a gas generator could save your life.

Above: The master bath provides a private refuge.
The bathtub, bench, and shelf are custom built of
reclaimed redwood. The counter is salvaged stone.

Right: The living room opens out to the landscape
beyond, providing a place of retreat and relaxation
all year.

Opposite: The guest bedroom is closed with a large
sliding track door of Douglas Fir and natural cotton.
When left open, guests are provided with a mesmer-
izing view of the mountains.

most of the two-plus bedroom home and studio. The nominal dimension lumber was locally milled and used for exterior siding, interior wall cladding, and ceilings. The dining room "lantern box" is built of locally and sustainably harvested Douglas fir, which was milled less than twenty-five miles away. The remaining walls are a veneer of natural plaster finish over Sheetrock. The wood floors, located in both bedroom wings, kitchen counters, and entry deck are made from Masaranduba, a sustainably grown and harvested wood from South America. Steel, with a recycled content of up to 60 percent, is used in many of the custom-fabricated details of the house and studio, not only because it is a readily available material in a rural environment but also due to its infinite recyclability.

The kitchen counter island, stair structures, guest bath counter support, sliding-door track, and custom door pivots were all fabricated on-site, reducing the need for secondary freight between place of purchase, shop fabrication, and location of final installation. The custom tub in the master bathroom as well as a shelf and bench are built of reclaimed redwood. Stone slabs were salvaged

An 1,800-kWh PV array, custom mounted to the shop, provides almost 50 percent of the electrical requirements for the house.

74

from a stone yard's discards for counters in both bathrooms.

While the home may appear remote, it is within seven miles of town and is adjacent to underground power, which made the hookup and a net-metering system feasible and beneficial for the larger energy requirements of a house, studio, and wood and welding shop. A fixed-panel PV array, which provides almost 50 percent of the electrical requirements for the house, is custom mounted to the shop. The electrical system is a grid intertie with no battery backup. Greater solar energy will be gained in the summer, leaving a minor gap in the amount of electrical production for the house in the winter. Thinking of future energy systems, and in order to take advantage of the constant wind conditions of the area, the installation of a wind turbine is under consideration; the wind turbine would cover 100 percent of the home and studio's electrical energy requirements, with the exception of the welding work that occurs in the shop.

Outside/In House AND STUDIO Strategies

Materials

- All appliances are Energy Star rated for their efficiency.
- Insulation in the walls and ceiling is Icynene, an open-cell system that is biodegradable and has minimal off-gassing.
- Wood siding, ceiling, and interior walls are locally milled Douglas fir.
- The roof and siding of part of the studio walls are galvanized metal, longer lasting than other roofing material and extremely durable in the extreme climate of Montana.
- Additional wall material is non-galvanized metal, which naturally rusts to a finished surface, requiring no additional sealant product.
- Additional interior wood detailing, including the dining room walls, inside and out, is a combination of reclaimed lumber and locally, sustainably harvested and milled Douglas fir.
- Wood floors, kitchen counters, and exterior decking is Masaranduba, a fast-growing, sustainably farmed and harvested wood from South America.
- The greenhouse window walls are built from wood windows reclaimed from the local post office during its renovation.
- Additional trim and detailing, including the kitchen island counter, back-splash, custom door pivots and trim, are steel, which is infinitely recyclable.
- The master bathtub, built-in bench and surround are made from reclaimed redwood.
- All non-wood walls are naturally pigmented plaster.

Passive Techniques

- Operable windows on both sides of the house allow summer winds to enter in and ventilate out to cool the house.
- Solar gain collected in the concrete slab during the winter radiates back out during the night to help keep the house warm.
- Water is collected in cisterns around the outside of the house to provide a variety of locations for irrigating.

Technologies

- The heating system is radiant in floor, heated by a gas boiler with a highly efficient heat exchanger for the domestic hot water use in the house.
- A 1,800-kW PV system by Isofoton (12 panels x 150 W) produces almost 100 percent of the home's and studio's electrical requirements.
- The inverter from Fronius transforms the solar energy from dc power to ac and is used in conjunction with a grid intertie setup for net metering.
- A gray-water system is installed for both bathrooms to provide water for the surrounding indigenous grasses and indigenous plant garden.
- A future domestic-scale wind turbine will be incorporated to allow the residence to operate fully off the grid when used in tandem with the PV panel and battery system.

At night, the dining room
glows like a lantern, casting
a glow onto the landscape.

As energy costs continue to rise for
natural gas and propane used for
heating and hot water in homes in
cold climates, a switch from gas to
electricity is not only feasible but will
minimize the reliance on nonrenewable energy resources

While not fully off the grid, the
Outside/In House serves as a working
model and laboratory for its designers
from which to explore alternative
energy and methods for resource
conservation. It is a model that can
be learned from, improved upon, and
integrated into future cold-weather
environments.

Hertz/Fong Residence

Venice, California ▪ Syndesis/David Hertz Architect ▪ 4,200 sq. ft.

The Hertz/Fong Residence is a dynamic interpretation of Southern California living. The mild weather that makes this area such a wonderful place to be outside plays a dominate role in the design and experience of this home through interior courtyards and living pavilions, which open up to the elements.

The original component of this residence, located within the compact neighborhood of Venice, was completed in 1996. The 2,700-square-foot home was comprised of two "pavilions"—one with the master bedroom above and the living spaces below, the other with two bedrooms above a garage for the children that could be reached through an enclosed "bridge" from the second floor of the master bedroom suite. Exterior balconies and fireplaces combined with small garden courtyards opened the house to the outside, creating the garden living for which California has become so famous.

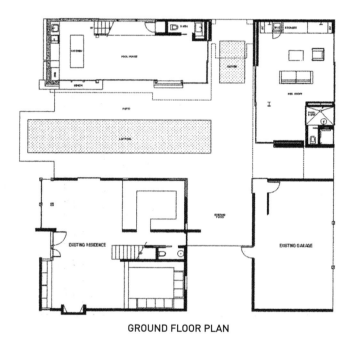

GROUND FLOOR PLAN

SECOND FLOOR PLAN

Although not originally anticipated, the family had the opportunity to expand the home when an adjacent lot came on the market. With the design of the second phase of the home, the potential to live life in a garden flanked by pavilions came into focus. At a minimal setback from the entry side of the home is a rammed-earth garden wall built of fly ash, decomposed granite sand, and cement. The wall provides a backdrop for a thin garden space filled with horsetail reeds and king palms. The street-side garden not only creates a beautiful buffer between the private

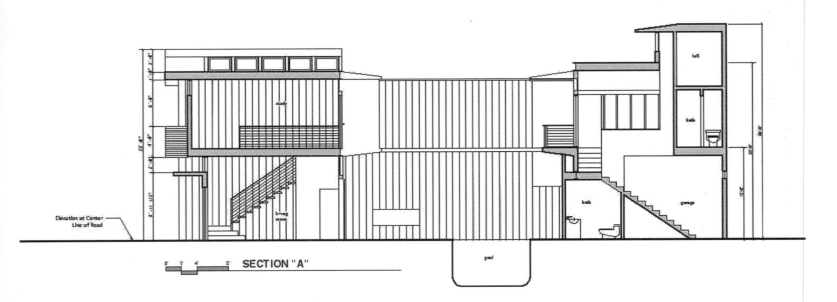

Elevation at Center
Line of Road

SECTION "A"

study

loft

bath

living
room

bath

garage

pool

court and the public street but also promises an even richer experience beyond the walled court. Completed in 2003, with a 1,500-square-foot addition, the home now focuses around a garden court, complete with lap pool and spa.

With the expansion of the home, two additional pavilions were created, each connected by second-level "bridges." The series of bridges, which connect all bedrooms and play areas for the children, allow the family to circulate at the private second level

Above, left: Louvers over windows at the second floor bridges provide a sun screen for the interior spaces.

Above, right: Rooms easily transition from interior to exterior and back to interior with the large sliding-glass doors that virtually erase the perimeters of enclosure.

Below, right: The new pool house has a kitchen that seamlessly blends with the details and cabinetry of the house, resulting in a space that feels more like an entertainment space than a service area.

Opposite: The custom wood stairs as well as the beam columns, trellis, and decks are all built from sustainable and reclaimed materials that include redwood, Ipe, and mahogany.

without going outside. Balconies and roof decks, an animated part of the outdoor experience, provide a sleeping porch, outside room with fireplace, and small greenhouse where orchids are grown. The home now provides four bedrooms and a master suite at the second level, along with a studio and game rooms for the kids. The ground floor has its original great room, living and dining rooms, plus a pool house with a new kitchen and recreation room and an additional bathroom for showering. Large sliding doors open onto the court, virtually erasing any separation between outside and in. Tropical plants, including black bamboo, giant timber bamboo, king palms, and horsetail reeds, which are easily adapted to the California climate, fill the garden areas of the courtyard. The resulting court space provides a magical place for spending time with the kids or relaxing.

The Hertz/Fong pool has a minimal impact on the environment. The pool's construction provides for both initial and long-term resource savings. Once the hole for the pool was made, it was lined with polystyrene foam, which insulates and helps retain the heat in the water. The pool serves as both a lap pool for exercise and a play area for the kids. Keeping the depth of the pool shallow, from 3 to 5 feet, reduces the overall amount of water that is required. The dark color of the pool walls helps to collect direct solar heat while a series of used RADCO commercial-grade solar hot-water panels heats the pool water through an open-loop system, which moves the water up to the solar panels and back again to the pool. The pool water heat is retained during the cool of the night with a tarp, which mechanically extends over the surface of the water. The pool filtration system replaces the chlorine with an ionization system that is chemical free.

Opposite and left: The court space in the center of the house brings together each of the living pavilions. The pool serves as both a lap pool for exercising and a play area for the kids. A solar hot-water heating system directly heats the water.

Above: The rammed-earth wall is enclosed with a glass-to-glass detail, only feasible in temperate climates.

Solar Hot-Water Systems

Solar water heaters are one of the most efficient alternative-energy systems due to the simplicity of the system and minimal "external" accessories required. Some manufacturers and suppliers claim that you can pay for your solar water collectors in energy savings in as little as two years. With the rising cost of energy, this claim could become a guaranteed fact.

In both the solar water heater and solar hot-water systems, a recirculating pump is required, which uses minimal energy. The choice of the system is typically determined by your climate. Solar hot-water systems operate through direct or indirect supply.

Direct Active System

If you live in a mild climate, you could easily employ what is called a direct active system. In this system domestic, potable water is brought directly into your house from your water supply. The water supply splits, with some serving cold water needs and some directed to the solar hot-water panels. As the water moves through the tubes in the panel, it is heated and sent to your hot-water tank. As you require, the solar-heated water is available for use.

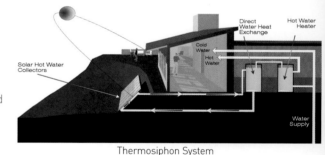

Thermosiphon System

Indirect System

If you live in a cold climate, where subfreezing weather is common in the winter, you would need to install an indirect system. In this system, solar-heated water is stored in the water storage tank. Instead of the hot water running through the tubes of the panels to collect heat, a liquid that has antifreeze characteristics (often this liquid is glycol) is used in the tubes that runs through a loop and the solar heat captured in the glycol is transferred to the water in your water-storage tank. This process is a simple heat-exchange concept.

Thermosiphon

If you have the opportunity to place your solar hot-water panels below the collection/recirculating point of your storage tank, you can employ a thermosiphon system that uses the heat of the liquid to build up the pressure of the liquid, which then moves and circulates without a pump. This system, which often places the panels at ground level to gain the proper relationship of solar collection to storage, will not work if the ground collects snow.

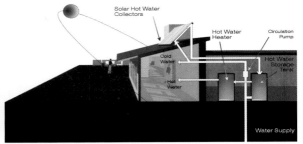

Direct Active System

Systems with Supplemental Sources

In both a direct active and indirect system, the temperature of the hot water that is gained from the sun may not be as hot as we are used to, or that we may need. Because of this, a hot-water heater is placed in line after the storage tank and before the hot water is released for your domestic use. While it may sound as though you are duplicating systems, it is the savings in overall energy generation that is the goal of these systems. The majority of the energy use for heating hot water occurs in the initial task of heating cold to warm or hot water. Using the sun for this task provides great savings for the overall heating of your domestic water.

There are some people who can live without the secondary tank. For the most part, these people live in very hot climates with long solar-gain days. To help retain heat, the storage tanks may be insulated like a thermos. The hot-water tank should be located as close to the panels as possible to reduce heat loss as the water travels from the panel to the storage tank.

Solar hot-water panels can also be used to generate the heat for a radiant-floor system as is used for the Hertz/Fong residence and Kashou/Caron residence. Both of these homes are located

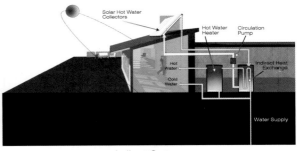

Indirect System

in a mild climate, which allows for the simple generation of the heat from the solar panels to work directly with the radiant systems. This system may require a secondary heat source (such as a boiler or hot-water tank) or secondary energy source in cold climates where storms most often bring cloudy days, thus reducing the ability to generate solar hot water.

With the rising cost of energy, and until the municipalities broaden, stabilize and consider the long-term source of energy; the various configurations of these systems can reduce the costs of your energy consumption and reduce your use of nonrenewable energy.

This page and opposite: Large sliding doors expand living experiences to the garden court. Concrete floors, with up to 40 percent fly ash in the mix, provide a sustainable and low-maintenance solution inside and out.

In addition to the home providing an almost Edenic experience, it is also easy on the environment. The concepts of sustainability play a large role in the design and construction of the home, making it a wonderful place to live, almost guilt free. A simple material palette of concrete, wood, and glass is employed throughout the house, further emphasizing a holistic experience of the home, inside and out. A conscientious effort was made to use sustainable wood throughout. Reclaimed, resawn Douglas fir timbers were used for roof beams, columns, and trellis members. The addition incorporates Forestry Stewardship Council –certified, sustainably harvested mahogany with FSC-certified Ipe (also called Paulope) hardwood used for the railings and stairs. Naturally pigmented wall and ceiling surfaces are complemented by Douglas fir used as both structure and trim, sealed with a low-VOC, clear finish.

Poured-in-place concrete, with up to 40 percent fly ash in the mix, was not only used for walls but also for furniture and floors. Battered concrete walls employed around the pool pavilion help to emphasize the openness to the court. Syndecrete, a sustainable concrete made with a combination of discarded recycled glass chips, computer products, and vinyl records as the aggregate, is used throughout the home as pool surround, floor pavers, countertops, and wall tiles as well as sink basins, tubs, showers, and fireplaces.

The active energy systems greatly reduce the home's reliance on the municipal energy system. According to Hertz, a 15 kW PV array connected as a grid intertie mounted on the roof provides 70-plus percent of the domestic house power. A solar

Above: A custom resin sink
shares space with a rinsing
shower for the pool. The
floor is made of Syndecrete
tiles and loose pebbles that
allow the shower water to
drain below them.

Right: An outdoor living
place is situated in an alcove
adjacent to the pool. A gas-
fired "flame" is reminiscent
of the casual bonfires made
on oceanside beaches.

Opposite: At night the house
glows, making apparent the
interwoven relationships
between inside and out,
ground and second floor,
including a large balcony off
of the children's playroom.

Hertz/Fong RESIDENCE Strategies

Passive Techniques

Solar hot-water heaters share rooftop space with PV panels.

- Large sliding-glass doors that open onto the courtyard, double doors, and operable windows all contribute to the passive cooling of the house.
- The dark color of the pool attracts solar gain, thus retaining heat in the pool.
- Concrete slab is used to retain the heat generated by the radiant-heat system.

Technologies

- A 15-kW Shell Solar PV Grid-Intertie system provides more than 70 percent of the energy for the house.
- The inverter is an SMA Sunny Boy.
- A used commercial-grade RADCO solar hot-water panel system heats the pool's water.
- A combined flat plate collector and evacuated parabolic collector panel system generates the hot water for both domestic use and radiant-heat floors.
- An ionizing/chemical-free system is used for filtrating the pool water.

Materials

- Sustainable wood used for beams, columns, trellis, decks, railing, and stairs includes reclaimed redwood, Ipe, and mahogany.
- Rammed-earth walls are made from a mixture of fly ash, decomposed granite sand, and 10 percent concrete.
- All concrete is made from a 40-percent high-volume fly ash mixture in partial substitution of Portland cement.
- Invented by the architect David Hertz, Syndecrete, a sustainable concrete product made with a combination of discarded recycled glass chips, computer products, and vinyl records as the aggregate forms the pool surround and patio, countertops, tiles, and sinks.
- The insulation is encapsulated glass wool in the walls and rigid polystyrene (EPS) in the roof, which uses no VOC in its manufacturing process.

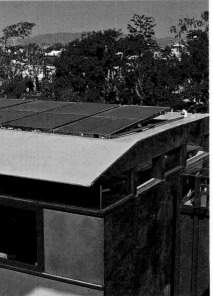

Left: The street-side entry to the house is enclosed with a rammed-earth wall, built from fly ash, decomposed granite sand, and cement. A thin garden space is filled with horsetail reeds and king palms.

Above: A series of PV panels on the roof are combined to create an array that produces 15 kW of power for the house.

hot-water system, using both flat plate collectors and an evacuated parabolic collector panel, generates the hot water for both domestic use and the radiant heat floors. Additional energy-saving strategies include automatic ventilating skylights and screened doors and windows, which allow for passive cooling of the home.

The Hertz/Fong Residence brings into focus strategies that may be adopted to create a home that is both relaxing and sustainable. Hot-water solar panels, PV arrays, and sustainable materials all remain in the background to the rich daily experiences of leisure of the home. In contrast to excesses and irresponsibility that we

have come to associate with lives of leisure, as was discussed in the introduction to the book, these homeowners can enjoy their home, knowing that it doesn't overly tax the Earth for their pleasure.

McDaniel Residence

Elk Creek Bluff, Manhattan, Montana ▪ Intrinsik Architecture ▪ 2,500 sq. ft.

Nestled into the saddle of a rising hill is the Elk Creek Bluff residence. To the northeast and below lies Elk Creek filled throughout the year with both migrating birds and full-time residents, which include bird, deer, fox, and rabbit. Red finches flutter around the many birdfeeders in the garden as they swing in the breeze. The visual landscape of the home is bounded by the distant Tobacco Root Mountains, the Flying D Ranch in the distance, and the immediate hills and creek, which provided direction for siting and views from within the home. For five years, the McDaniels lived in a guesthouse they built on the site prior to embarking on the design of the main house. With the years spent on the site, one issue had

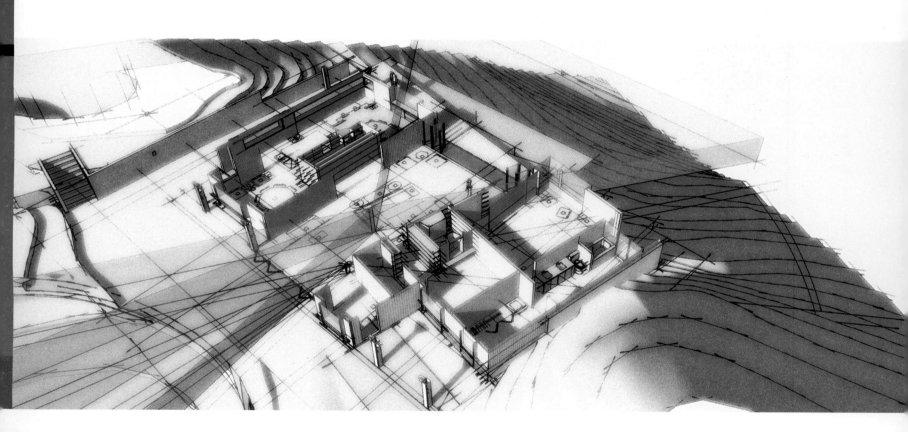

become abundantly clear to them and became a primary instigator for the design of the new house: the wind blows almost constantly across this landscape. There is seldom a gentle breeze in the winter. At times the wind coming from the south and southwest gusts more than 60 miles per hour. The condition of the wind had often deterred the McDaniels'

interaction outside, an aspect of living they hoped to improve upon with the new home.

The McDaniels also wanted to build as sustainably as possible, incorporating reclaimed materials of construction, solar energy for day lighting and geothermal energy for their heat system and domestic hot water. In this cold and windy climate,

heat can be the primary energy draw in residences. The great perk of a geothermal system is high energy efficiency. With energy prices on the rise, the efficiency of the geothermal system, in this case used for radiant-floor heat, can pay for itself in four years, not to mention the natural resources it can conserve. The geothermal system installed at the

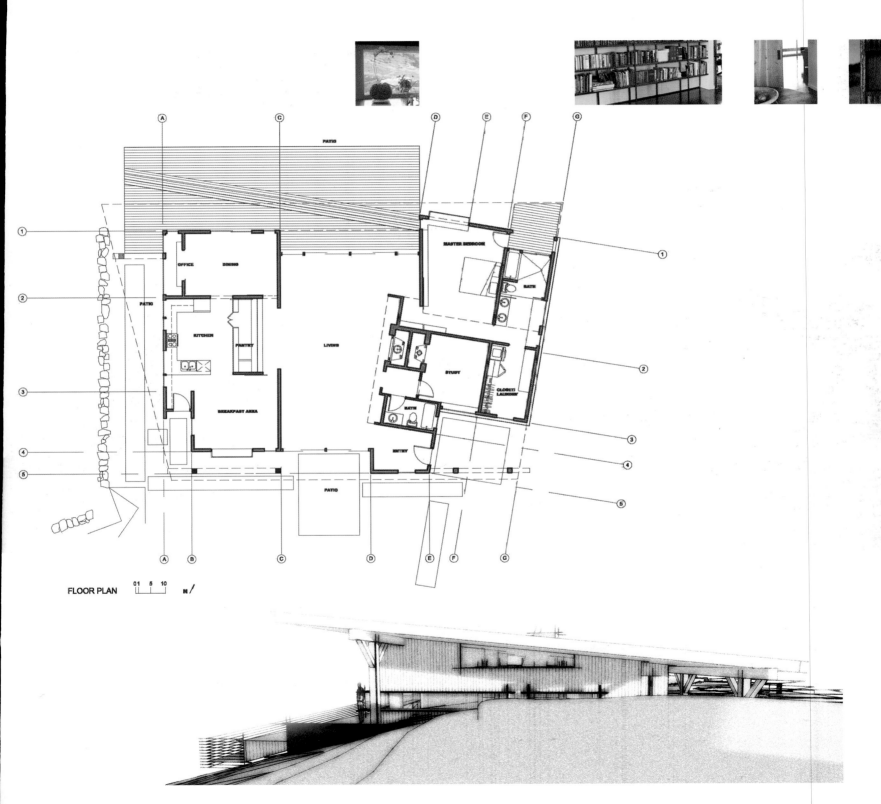

FLOOR PLAN

Left: An outdoor breezeway built of reclaimed timbers provides protection from the wind and a passage to the deck space.

Opposite: Views of Elk Creek below provide a great place to watch wildlife.

Above: The house acts as a wind block for the larger exterior deck from the living room, allowing the home-owners to extend their living from inside and out.

McDaniels' home is referred to as a horizontal closed-loop system. With a geothermal, or ground-source unit, the relative constant temperature of the ground (44 degrees in this area of Montana) is accessed by installing a closed loop in the form of a loop field into the ground that is filled with an antifreeze and water mixture to exchange heat between the ground and the geothermal heat pump. In the winter, this heat pump takes low-temperature heat from the loop field and turns it, using the standard heat-pump refrigeration cycle, into high-temperature heat to be used within the home. This heat pump, located in the mechanical room, transfers the high-temperature heat to a standard radian-heat floor-system loop as well as supplements the domestic hot water through the use of an integral desuperheater. When it is hot outside, the same system can be reversed with the warmth of the house drawn into the system and exchanged with the cool ground temperature, keeping the house cool. The summer heat

Left: The master bathroom has an extra large walk-in shower "room," with a sliding door and deck beyond that creates a seamless experience of living as one can shower or take a bath while enjoying the views of the landscape beyond.

Above: Custom-made surface mounted sliding doors built of steel and reclaimed wood provide openness or privacy between the rooms.

Opposite, left: A library wall of books in the living room also serves as a transition space to kitchen and dining rooms. The polished and stained concrete floor provides radiant heat.

Opposite, right: A large sliding door opens the kitchen area into the living room, providing views to Elk Creek below.

exchange results in a by-product of "free heat" provided to the domestic hot-water heater.

Dan Harding, the designer and principal of Intrinsik Architecture, took to heart the McDaniels' requests. A series of studies and an analysis of the site were employed to understand wind direction, solar orientation, and views. The scheme that resulted centers an open primary living space at the low point of the saddle, flanked by the more solid volumes of the bedrooms to the east and kitchen and dining room to the west that act as wind breaks and protection for both inside and outside spaces. The center living space opens on both ends with sliding glass doors to provide pavilion-like living during the warm months and passive solar heat gain in the concrete slab during the winter, as well as dynamic views to the distant mountains and Elk Creek below. The house itself creates

Geothermal Systems

Advantages and Options

Geothermal, or ground-source systems, use the constant temperature of the Earth, which generally holds at fifty-five degrees, or water to heat or cool a building or to heat water. During the winter, the system absorbs the heat from the ground and uses it to heat the home. In the warmer months, heat is removed from the home by reversing the process, transferring it back to the ground. These systems can be used in any locale, from urban to remote. They can be used in conjunction with other systems, such as hot-water storage tanks, hot-water heaters, and forced-air systems to produce radiant heat, forced-air cooling, and hot water.

The advantage of a ground-source system is that it greatly reduces the amount of energy required to run the mechanical system, which reduces the day-to-day costs of heating and cooling your house. This can make a difference if you are on or off the grid. If you are connected to the grid's gas or electricity, it can reduce your energy requirements by three to four times what a conventional gas-fired or electrical system would cost. If you are living off the grid, it reduces the amount of propane or PV generation required, also saving money and resources.

As this book is being written, the United States has experienced a huge rise in the cost of energy. Many speculators say the rise in energy cost will not recede. With these rate increases, as much as 40 percent in some states, the ground-source system can pay for itself in energy savings (resource savings, too) in a shorter period of time. In the past year, the payoff period of

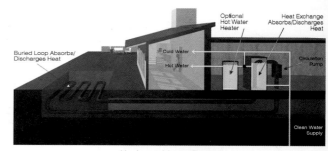

Horizontal Loop System

such a system that is run from natural gas has gone from seven to four years. If you are running your mechanical system from electricity or propane, the payoff period is virtually immediate. Additionally, these systems have a long life and require little maintenance, with compressor replacement rated at twenty years or more.

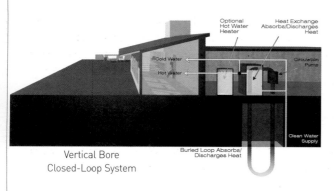

Vertical Bore
Closed-Loop System

Closed or Open Loop

There are two basic types of geothermal systems: closed and open loop. The closed loop relies on the temperature of the earth transferred as a heat exchange through a coil filled with antifreeze (glycol or methanol, which are both biodegradable) into a heat-pump system. The closed loop can be run horizontally or vertically into the ground. The horizontal or vertical direction of the loop is primarily determined by your environment. If you have enough land that is not rocky, a pit or trenches can be dug in which to place the loop field. If you have limited space, multiple vertical bores can be made for the coil loops. The depth of the field and vertical bore is determined by locale (which affects the ground temperature) and soil type. Typically, the horizontal field installation costs less than the vertical bore installation.

A new system on the market is a "slinky loop," which uses wider horizontal trenches with tubes that are coiled in a closed-loop application. The concept of this system is that you can use the coiled tube to collect and transfer the ground temperature in less space while still using the less expensive ground-trenching method.

An open-loop system is typically the most cost effective of all of the geothermal installations if you have the ideal soil conditions and well or ground water. This open-loop system draws from a water well, which is then discharged back into the ground, rather than a self-contained loop system filled with antifreeze. The well water never comes in contact with the "antifreeze" loop of the heat pump located in the mechanical space, and therefore can be released back into the ground without affecting the condition/quality of the water. This is a common retrofit system in rural locations where a ground well is available.

Pond/lake loops are also an economical source for "ground" temperature. If you live in an environment with a pond or lake that is deep enough to not freeze through in the winter or has enough water in it to retain the temperature of the Earth, rather than heat up in the summer, you have a source that retains "ground" temperature without the need to excavate. With this system, the loops are placed on the bottom of the lake or pond, which acts as the heat transfer location.

How They Work

The geothermal closed-loop system works by transferring the ground temperature into the antifreeze liquid of the tube, serving as a "heat exchanger." An open-loop system uses water as the heat-exchange system with the heat pump. Heat exchange works through vapor compression created with a heat pump located in your mechanical space by placing the liquid under pressure and consequently generating enough heat energy to change the ground-loop tube temperature to 160 to 180 degrees Fahrenheit. This temperature is then transferred to an interior "closed"-tube loop of the heat pump into various home uses, such as hot water or radiant heat. The system can be reversed to produce cool air for a forced-air, evaporative, or radiant system.

While ground-source energy (a geothermal system) may sound complicated, it is very simple, highly economical, and available through a variety of geothermal or ground-source-system installers.

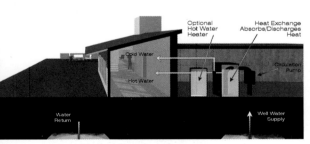

Vertical Bore Open System

a wind block for a large deck that extends from the living room to the dining room, cascading out over the creek below, providing a view and experience of the landscape as it changes through the seasons. A smaller deck, which extends from the master bathroom, offers a private outdoor refuge. A simple, low-lying shed roof covers the home and some

exterior spaces, keeping the overall volume of the home modest and wed to its site. Reclaimed timbers, plank wood, and corrugated metal serve as siding for the home. A built-up gravel roof is used to blend the roof surface into the surrounding rocky, high-desert landscape.

The interior of the home has a casualness to it with nonstructural

walls held down from the ceiling and finely crafted details of steel and reclaimed wood incorporated into sliding doors, bookshelves, and a fire-place surround. Specific orientation of windows and openings frame the landscape like large painted canvases or intimate vignettes. The walls and ceiling of the home are finished in a palette of white, which contrasts with

Opposite: Reclaimed corrugated steel is used for the exterior siding. Window trim is fabricated from 60 percent recycled-content steel, making the exterior of the home low maintenance, long lived, and recyclable.

Left: The kitchen brings in natural light through a continuous window that replaces the backsplash without losing upper cabinet storage space.

Above: The custom fabricated steel fireplace surround provides a beautiful focal point in the living room.

the dark brown–stained concrete slab. The ceiling is finished with white-washed short plank aspen, which creates a lightness above the grounded floor.

While the McDaniel Residence does not incorporate a fully off-the-grid energy system, it demonstrates the ability to considerably reduce our reliance on grid energy and conserve resources through the thoughtful integration of a highly efficient, Earth-reliant energy system. Geothermal strategies for heating and cooling are among the oldest known to us and remain some of the most efficient systems on the market. The concept for the various geothermal systems is the same; however, using the thermal qualities of the Earth to save resources, the strategies of application are different. The type of system is typically determined by the environmental conditions of the home, including amount of available ground for the loop installation, available ground water, and the conditions of the soil. For the McDaniels, who have abundant land but not abundant water, a closed-loop system is the most practical. (See geothermal diagrams on pages 102–3 for additional systems.) The highly efficient heating system used in this house, integrated with its highly efficient wall and roof insulation, make a transition to a PV system for electrical requirements a simple and achievable next step.

McDaniel RESIDENCE Strategies

Materials

- Icynene insulation is used in walls and ceilings.
- The perimeter of the floor slab is insulated in order to prevent extensive heat loss.
- Reclaimed metal is used for exterior siding.
- Reclaimed wood is used for exterior siding, interior doors, and book-shelves.
- Short-length board aspen is used as the ceiling material throughout the house. Harvesting aspen is believed to be a resource-sensitive process because the harvesting of trees does not destroy the overall root system, allowing for continual regrowth without the need for replanting or reforesting.
- Steel with a 60-percent reclaimed content, fabricated by Intrinsik Architecture, is used for details that include the bookshelf frames, sliding-door frames, fireplace surround, and exterior window trim conditions.

Passive Techniques

- Passive cooling is created in the center living space from large sliding glass doors on both ends. Additional cooling occurs through multiple operable windows throughout the rest of the house, which can ventilate out through the living room.
- Using the volume of the house as a foil against the significant winds throughout the year not only increases the owner's time outside in the spaces sheltered by the home, it also reduces the degree of cold-air filtration in the winter through the house by minimizing the window sizes in the windward walls.

Technologies

- Geothermal system is a Econar GW771 Ultra Hydronic Heat-Pump rated at 7 nominal tons with integral domestic hot-water desuperheater.
- Seven 3/4" High-Density Poly-Ethylene (HDPE) 3/4" coils.
- Eighty-gallon buffer tank (standard eighty-gallon electric water heater also used for emergency and construction heat).
- Circulating pumps for ground loop and buffer tank loop.
- Standard 3-zone hydronic control system with single hydronic circulating pump.
- Loop field consists of 7 trenches dug to a depth of roughly 7 feet using a 3-foot bucket on a track hoe. Each HDPE coil was placed in the trench using a slinky overlap design, placing 800 feet of coil within a 100-foot trench. The trenches were then reverse-return headered using one 1/4" HDPE pipe and connected directly to the heat-pump system. The soils of the site are a very compact clay-sand-loam mixture with moderate to low moisture levels.

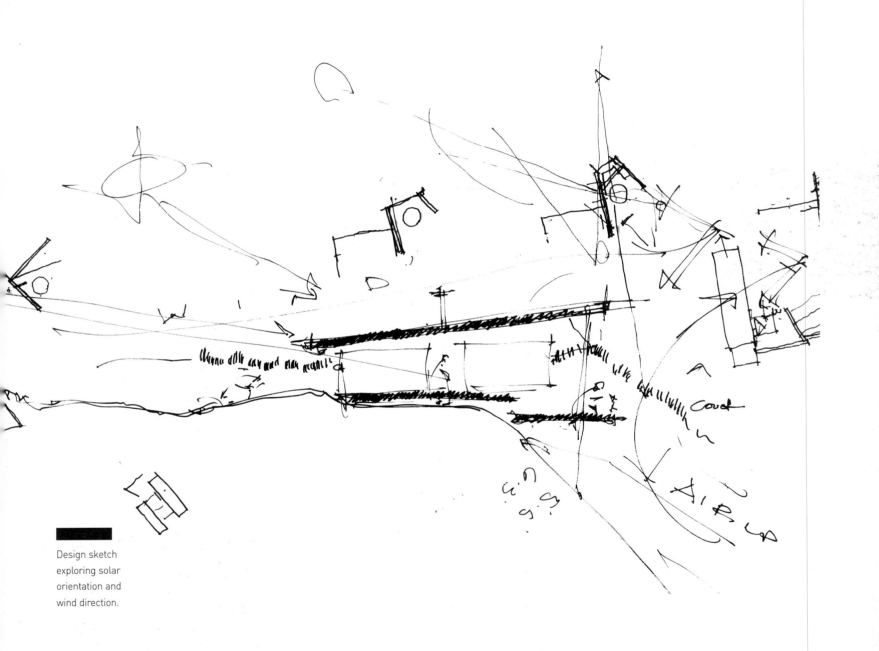

Design sketch
exploring solar
orientation and
wind direction.

Kashou/Caron Residence

Ukiah, California • Arkin/Tilt Architects • 1,410 sq. ft.

Ukiah, California, is located north of San Francisco amidst an agricultural landscape of rolling hills dotted with oak trees. It is a world apart from the urban life of the nearby city. In Ukiah, people can reflect upon the rhythms of the land and actively engage in a rural lifestyle. While this may sound like a bucolic dreamscape, the Kashou/Caron residence, located west of Ukiah down a rural dirt road, does not merely provide a weekend retreat. Rather the house and the land it sits on provide the opportunity for an active alternative lifestyle. An organic heritage fruit orchard helps to set the pace of the home life and immediately launches owners and visitors into the consideration of living off the land. The remoteness of the homesite not only

112

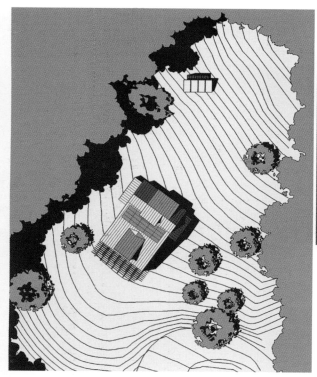

SITE PLAN

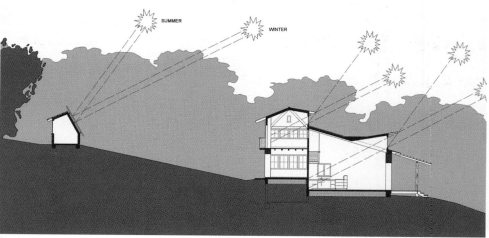

SECTION

suggests its independence but requires it. With no municipal ties available, the Kashou/Caron residence operates fully off the grid.

The home's independence from municipal energy is gained through a series of strategies. A PV system, which generates approximately 1,050 kWh, is mounted to the southern face of the roof of the house with additional energy stored in a battery bank for use during poor solar days and nights. Backup heat is provided by a gas-fired system. A solar hot-water system, located on the roof of the adjacent shed, serves a dual purpose, providing heat to the deep sand bed radiant system as well as domestic hot water. Water is pumped from a well and stored in a cistern for domestic use, orchard irrigation, and fire suppression. The pump for the well and cistern is activated by a direct-fed PV panel.

The house is lent a vernacular voice through both its proportions and materials of construction. But rather

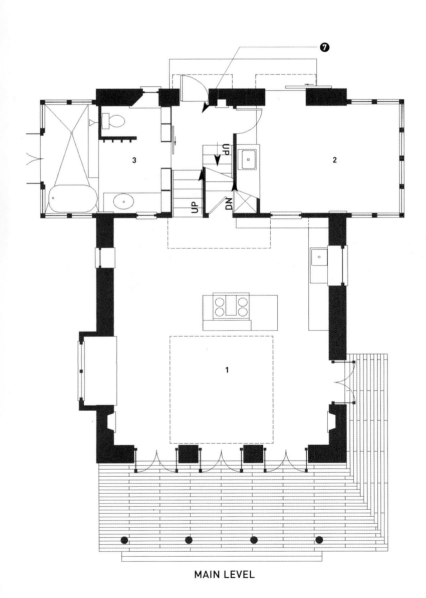

MAIN LEVEL

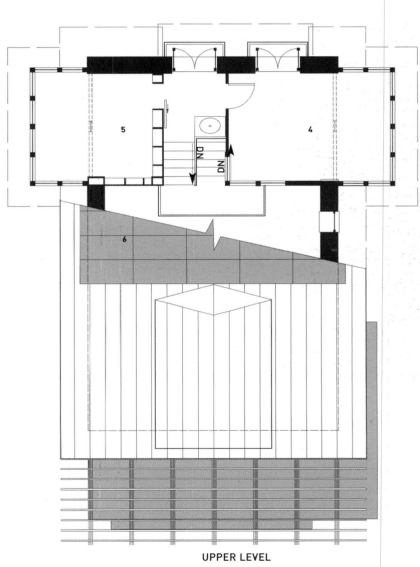

UPPER LEVEL

0 2 4 6 8 10 FEET

Left: A series of french doors and operable celestory windows work together to naturally ventilate and cool the house.

Above: A series of PV panels mounted directly to the roof of the house provide all of the electrical energy requirements for the house.

than fall into the nostalgic traps of the traditional formal characteristics of the local vernacular, the home's design starts from this heritage and is crafted into a highly particular assembly that is both contemporary in its nature and playful in its nods to its vernacular language. Details of construction and material bring an asceticism to the sense of the house, a matter-of-fact humility to the place. Primary entry into the house occurs over the root cellar, fitting within the slope of the land. An open stairway, with internal balcony, rises from entry level to second floor. Small, but particular, the main floor of the home is a double-height open space, which centers around the activity of harvesting and preparing food. The root cellar is easily accessed from the kitchen below the central stair court. Salvaged interior windows playfully connect the private spaces to the public, creating the sense of an Italian piazza in the great room, while also opening through the

Left: Reclaimed wood is used for exterior siding along with a colored clay finish over the straw bale infill wall system.

Below: Solar hot-water panels mounted to the adjacent shed provide domestic hot water and heat for the radiant floor system.

Above: South-facing french doors bring light and solar heat into the house in the winter. The light and heat are blocked in the summer by the porch trellis.

Right: Reclaimed, salvaged, and refurbished materials and fixtures, such as doors, windows, countertops, and kitchen fixtures and appliances, give the house a distinct character as well as save artifacts from filling landfills.

Far right: Operable interior windows from the second-floor bedrooms allow the house to ventilate by creating a crossbreeze through the house.

Opposite: Concrete floors with radiant heat warm the house while highly insulative straw bale walls help to retain the temperature inside.

house to increase ventilation. Orientation toward the south allows airflow and daylight through a series of glass french doors onto a patio with developing vines on a trellis canopy. Passive solar gain and heat release is provided through the clerestory windows in the modified dormer windows above the dining and kitchen area and the open stairway to the second-floor bedrooms. Private spaces, which include bedrooms, bathrooms, and a creative room for various art projects are stacked over one another, minimizing the footprint of the home. Views across the landscape are gained through operable windows joined together in series in these rooms. Exterior balconies from the stair court and master bedroom open onto the surrounding orchard, maximizing the amount of ventilation that can be drawn through the house.

Along with alternative energy, sustainable materials and fixtures are a key focus of the home. The primary system of construction is hay/bale infill, finished inside and out with a sprayed and hand-troweled earth

Left: Reclaimed bathroom fixtures are combined with reclaimed wood for the walls and ceiling, providing a sense of history to the home.

Above: The thickness of the straw bale walls, finished with hand-troweled earth from the site, allows for niches to be built into the thickness of the wall.

Opposite, left: Window seats provide an additional sitting area for the living room and makeshift sleeping alcove for guests.

Opposite, right: The main bedroom feels like a tree house with wraparound windows on three sides. Reclaimed wood provides material for both ceiling and floors.

harvested from the site. Wood-framed exterior walls are insulated with denim batt and clad with salvaged redwood, cedar siding, or interior gypsum board finished with Alis (a colored clay). The roof is AEP-Span Standing Seam with Zincalume finish. The concrete floor is sealed and waxed. All plumbing fixtures, interior windows and doors, and stove are salvaged and refurbished. Cabinetry, wood ceiling, second-floor system, stairs, and trim are re-milled and crafted of a variety of salvaged woods, including redwood, fir, and oak, which give a warmth and depth to the interior finishes.

The Kashou/Caron residence provides a retreat from city life and also a reminder of what is possible when we are attentive to the place in which we live. Independence from the grid can allow for an interdependence with the world that we can spend a lifetime learning from and enjoying.

Kashou/Caron RESIDENCE Strategies

Passive Techniques

- The house is oriented for passive solar heating in the concrete slab, occurring through the south-facing glass doors.
- The house is designed for flow-through passive cooling as breezes enter from the south through the bottom-floor glass doors and clerestory windows and exit out the open doors and windows at the second floor. Additional ventilation potential is created with interior windows at the second floor that open onto the living space below.

Technologies

- A 1,050 kW BP PV system (7 panels x 150 W) produce virtually 100 percent of the home's power.
- The PV panels are mounted to the roof with a PSP fast-track system.
- The inverter is a Vanner 3,500-W panel.
- A C-40 Charge Controller has a Tri-Metric 20/20 meter.
- The transfer switch is an IOTA ATS30.
- Twelve 85G-21 battery bank is employed for 1,045 Ah of storage at 24 V.
- Solar hot water is generated with four 4 x 10 Heliodyne hot-water collectors.

Materials

- Main Walls: on-edge straw bales between vertical I-joists, with troweled, sprayed earth using soil from the site.
- Secondary Walls: frame walls with recycled denim insulation and salvaged redwood, cedar siding, or gypsum board with Alyss finish (interior walls).
- Salvaged Douglas fir is used for the stair slabs.
- Salvaged Douglas fir and redwood are used for the trim throughout the house.
- Salvaged interior doors and windows are from local suppliers.
- Salvaged and refurbished plumbing fixtures are used.
- Reclaimed and reused butcher-block countertop are from an oak bowling return lid.
- Energy-saving appliances include a salvaged and refurbished stove, refrigerator by Sunfrost, and Bosch washing machine.
- Alis, an interior clay-based wall finish with no petroleum products or VOC from Vital Systems is used throughout the house.

Projects at a Glance

PROJECT	ARCHITECT/DESIGNER	LOCATION	SIZE	OFF THE GRID	INTERTIE
URBAN					
Hertz/Fong Residence	Syndesis	Venice, CA	4,200 sf		X
Capitol Hill House	Blip Design	Seattle, WA	4,200 sf		X
RURAL					
Ryker/Nave Residence	Ryker/Nave Design	Livingston, MT	2,100 sf		X
McDaniel Residence	Intrinsik Architecture	Manhattan, MT	2,500 sf		
Bruny Island Guesthouse	1+2 Architecture	Bruny Island, Tasmania, Australia	2,150 sf	X	
Kashou/Caron Residence	Arkin/Tilt Architects	Ukiah, CA	1,440 sf	X	

Sources of Reference

Sources Used and References

Lawrence, Robin Griggs. "The Godparents of Green," *Natural Home*, May/June 2000, 44–51.

LeBlanc, Sydney. "Sustainability in Stages," *Dwell*, Vol. 6, December/January 2006, 69–76.

Lerner, Steve. *Eco-Pioneers: Practical Visionaries Solving Today's Environmental Problems.* Cambridge, MA: The MIT Press, 1997.

Ludwig, Art. *Builder's Greywater Guide*. Santa Barbara: Oasis Design, 1995.

Pijawka, K. David, and Kim Shetter. *The Environment Comes Home: Arizona Public Service's Environmental Showcase Home.* Tempe: The University of Arizona Press, 1995.

McCoy, Esther. *Case Study Houses: 1945–1962*. Santa Monica: Hennessey + Ingalls, 1977.

Stein, Benjamin, and John S. Reynolds. *Mechanical and Electrical Equipment for Buildings.* 9th ed. New York: John Wiley and Sons, Inc., 2000.

Strong, Steven J. *The Solar Electric House*. MA: Sustainability Press, 1993.

Wines, James. *Green Architecture.* Koln, Germany: Taschen, 2000.

Web Sites Referenced

www.alliantenergygeothermal.com

www.bfi.org

www.eere.energy.gov

www.eere.energy.gov/solar/

www.justgeothermal.com

www.nrel.gov

www.pbs.org/fmc/segments/progseg9.htm

www.sandia.gov

www.waterfurnace.com

BACKUP	WATER COLLECTION	GEOTHERMAL	SOLAR ENERGY	SOLAR H20	GRAY WATER
			X	X	
X	X		X	X	
	X		X		X
		X			
X	X		X		X
X			X	X	

Photo Credits

Page 14: Todd Jersey, architect; Audrey Hall, photographer

Page 20, above right: Todd Jersey, architect; Audrey Hall, photographer

Pages 23, 24: Scott Frances, photographer

Page 26: Paul Bardagiy

Page 27, left: Pliny Fisk; right, Kit Morris

Pages 28, 31: Scot Zimmerman

Pages 34–45: photos of Bruny Island guesthouse, Peter Hyatt, photographer

Architects, Designers, Builders, and Technicians

Bruny Island Guesthouse
Architect
1+2 Architecture Pty., Ltd
31 Melville St.
Hobart, Tasmania 7000
Australia
Tel. 03 6234 8122
Fax 03 6234 8211
www.1plus2architecture.com

Project Team: Cath Hall, Fred Ward, Mike Verdouw

Landscape Architecture
1+2 Architecture Pty., Ltd

Structural Engineers
Gandy & Roberts Pty., Ltd
159 Davey St.
Hobart, Tasmania 7000
Australia

Service Engineers
SEMF Holdings Pty. Ltd.
45 Murray St.
Hobart, Tasmania 7000
Australia

General Contractor
John Hebblewhite
62 Queen St.
Sandy Bay, Tasmania 7000
Australia

Alternative Energy Technical Supplier
Rob Wells
Power Plus
25 Derwent Park Rd.
Derwent Park, Tasmania 7009
Tel. 03 6272 4366

Capitol Hill House
Architect
Jim Burton
BLIP design
3235 42nd Ave. W
Seattle, WA 98199
Tel. 206.501.8746
www.blipdesign.com

Structural Engineer
Swenson Say Faget
2124 Third Ave., Ste. 100
Seattle, WA 98121
Tel. 206.443.6212
www.swensonsayfaget.com

General Contractor
McGinnis Construction
3220 198th St. South
SeaTac, WA 98188
Tel. 206.227.9086

Technical Supplier/Installation
Photovoltaics Consultant
Northwest Solar Center
7400 NE Sand Point Way
Seattle, WA 98115
Tel. 206.396.8446
www.northwestsolarcenter.org

Photovoltaic
Sound Power
29931 NE 190th St.
Duvall, WA 98019
Tel. 425.844.8748
www.soundpower.us

Radiant Floor and Solar Hot Water
Advanced Radiant Technology
2821 NW Market St.
Seattle, WA 98107
Tel. 206.783.4315
www.advancedradiant.com

"Smart House" (data, low voltage)
Coast to Coast Technologies
14242 Ambaum Blvd SW, Ste. 4
Seattle, WA 98166
Tel. 360.440.4350
c2ctech@comcast.net

Center for Maximum Potential Building Systems
Pliny Fisk and Gail Vittori
8604 FM 969
Austin, TX 78724
Tel. 512.928.4786
Fax 512.926.4418
www.cmpbs.org

Environmental Showcase Home
Jones Studio
4450 N. 12th St., Ste. 104
Phoenix, AZ 85014
Tel. 602.264.2941
Fax 602.264.3440
www.jonesstudioinc.com

Hertz/Fong Residence
Architect
Syndesis, Inc.
David Hertz, AIA, Architect
2908 Colorado Ave.
Santa Monica, CA 90404
Tel. 310.829.9932
Fax 310.829.5641
www.syndesisinc.com

General Contractor
Syndesis, Inc.
David Hertz, AIA, Architect
2908 Colorado Ave.
Santa Monica, CA 90404
Tel. 310.829.9932
Fax 310.829.5641
www.syndesisinc.com

Structural Engineer
C. W. House and Associates
3347 Motor Ave., Ste. 200
Los Angeles, CA 90043
Tel. 310.838.0383
Fax 310.838.5380
www.cwhowe.com

Technical Supplier/Installation
Radiant Heat
Dexters Solar Radiant Energy Services
PO Box 41924
Santa Barbara, CA 93140
Tel. 805.884.5188
Fax 877.331.4094
dexsolrad@cox.net

Pool Solar Hot Water
All Valley Solar
valleysolar@earthlink.net

Photovoltaic System
Three Phases Solar
(no longer in business)

Kashou/Caron Residence
Architect
Arkin/Tilt Architects
1101 8th St., #180
Berkeley, CA 94710
Tel. 510.528.9830
www.arkintilt.com

Structural Engineer
Kevin Donahue
1101 8th St., #180
Berkeley, CA 94710

General Contractor
Fred Sly
75 N. Main St., #194
Willits, CA 95490

Vital Systems
PO Box 751
Ukiah, CA 95482
Tel. 888.859.6336
www.vitalsystems.net

Technical Supplier
Solar Hot Water
Artha Renewable Energy
9784 County Rd. K
Amherst, WI 54406
Tel. 715.824.3463
www.wi-net.com

Photovoltaic Energy
Advance: Solar, Hydro, Wind,
Power Company
6291 N. State St.
PO Box 23
Calpelle, CA 95418
Tel. 707.458.0588

McDaniel Residence
Architect
Intrinsik Architecture, Inc.
428 E. Mendenhall
Bozeman, MT 59715
Tel. 406.582.8988
Fax 406.582.8911
www.intrinsikarchitecture.com

Principal in Charge, Designer: Dan
Harding
Project Team: Gayle Mauer, Travis
Growney, Henri Fochs, Travis
Mandeville, Tyson Holland

General Contractor
Intrinsik Architecture, Inc.
Principal in Charge: Dan Harding

Geothermal System
Michael Ketcham
Building Energy Solutions, Inc
2850 Bear Canyon Rd.
Bozeman, MT 59715
Tel. 406.522.0033
ketcham@imt.net

Monier House
Kimberly Ackert
Ackert Architecture
400 E. 55th St.
New York, NY 10022
Tel. 212.832.3603
Fax 646.521.0367
www.ackertarchitecture.com

Outside/In House
Designer
Ryker/Nave Design
13 Cokedale Spur
Livingston, MT 59047
Tel. 406.222.7488
Fax 406.222.7488
www.rykernave.com

Principals in Charge: Brett Nave and
Lori Ryker
Design team: Brett Nave, Lori Ryker,
Ciaran Fitzgerald, Patricia Flores

General Contractor
RN Construction
13 Cokedale Spur
Livingston, MT 59047
Tel. 406.222.7488
Fax 406.222.7488
www.rykernave.com

Principal in Charge: Brett Nave
Build Team: Ciaran Fitzgerald,
Patricia Flores, Lori Ryker, Joe
Roodell, Grif Heath, Pat Dunbaker,
Lincoln Jamrog, Jamie Slagel, Brett
Hunter, Wayne Sellers, Jason
Cipriani, Mark McPhie

Technical Supplier
Photovoltaic Energy
Energy Outfitters, Ltd.
Paul Farley
543 NE "E" St.
Grants Pass, OR 97526
Tel. 541.476.4200
Fax 541.476.7480

Off-the-Grid Technology Resources

Geothermal Heat Equipment Manufacturers*

ClimateMaster
www.climatemaster.com

FHP Manufacturing
www.fhp-mfg.com

The Trane Company
www.trane.com

WaterFurnace International
www.waterfurnace.com

Advanced Geothermal Technology
dcreyts@advgeo.com

American Geothermal, Inc.
www.amgeo.com

Earth To Air Systems, Inc.
www.earthtoair.com

ECR Technologies
www.ecrtech.com

*From Geoexchange:
www.geoexchange.org/local/manufacturers.htm

Photovoltaic Manufacturers*
BP Solar
www.bp.com/modularhome.do?categoryId=4320&contentId=7004540

Evergreen Solar Panels
www.evergreensolar.com

GE Energy Solar Panels
www.gepower.com/prod_serv/products/solar/en/index.htm

Global Solar Energy
www.globalsolar.com

Isofoton Solar Panels
www.isofoton.com

Kyocera
www.kyocerasolar.com/products/ksimodule.html

Matrix Solar
www.matrixsolar.com

Mitsubishi Electric
global.mitsubishielectric.com/bu/solar/index.html

RWE SCHOTT Solar
www.rweschottsolar.com

Sanyo
www.sanyo.com/industrial/solar

Sharp
solar.sharpusa.com/solar

Shell/Siemens
www.shell.com/home/Framework?siteId=shellsolar

SunWize
www.sunwize.com

Uni-Solar
www.uni-solar.com

*From Affordable Solar
www.affordable-solar.com

Small Wind Turbine Manufacturers*
Abundant Renewable Energy
www.abundantre.com

Bergey Windpower Co.
www.bergey.com

Entegrity Wind Systems
www.entegritywind.com

Energy Maintenance Service
www.energyms.com

Lorax Energy
www.lorax-energy.com
Northern Power Systems
www.northernpower.com

Solar Wind Works
www.solarwindworks.com

Southwest Windpower Co.
www.windenergy.com

Wind Turbine Industries Corp.
www.windturbine.net

*From American Wind Energy Association:
www.awea.org/faq/smsyslst.html

Solar Hot-Water Equipment Manufacturers*

ACR Solar International Corporation
www.solarroofs.com

FAFCO, Inc.
www.fafco.com

Harter Industries, Inc.
www.harterindustries.com

Heliocol
www.heliocol.com

Heliodyne, Inc.
www.heliodyne.com

JED Engineering, Inc.
www.jedengineering.com

Solahart
www.solahart.com.au

SunEarth, Inc.
www.sunearthinc.com

Thermo Dynamics, Ltd.
www.thermo-dynamics.com

Thermo Technologies
www.thermomax.com

Alternate Energy Technologies, LLC
www.aetsolar.com

*From Solar Rating & Cert. Corp. (SRCC):
solar-rating.org

Index

128